PESHUTO SHEL
MIKRA

Selected Ma'amarim from the Writings of
Harav Yehuda Copperman, zt"l

MOSAICA PRESS

PESHUTO SHEL MIKRA

פשוטו של מקרא

Selected Ma'amarim from the Writings of

HaRav Yehuda Copperman, zt"l

On the occasion of his first yahrzeit,
the 23rd of Tevet, 5777

Adapted into English by Immanuel Bernstein

Mosaica Press, Inc.
© 2017 by Mosaica Press
Designed and typeset by Brocha Mirel Strizower

Published and distributed by:
Mosaica Press, Inc.
www.mosaicapress.com
info@mosaicapress.com

TABLE OF CONTENTS

TRANSLATOR'S PREFACE

IT IS WITH much joy and gratitude to HaKadosh Baruch Hu that we make a selection of the *ma'amarim* of Rav Yehuda Copperman, *zt"l*, on his beloved subject of *peshuto shel mikra* available in English as we approach the occasion of his first *yahrzeit*.

About the Translation

Although English was his mother tongue, and he gave many regular *shiurim* and *chugim* in English, Rav Copperman wrote almost only in Hebrew. In adapting the *ma'amarim* into English, we have tried to remain faithful to his original style but emphasized clarity and comprehensibility over literacy of translation.

Some guidelines regarding the translation:

Sources

- *Pesukim* and quotations from Chazal and Rashi are presented both in Hebrew and English.
- Quotations from other *mefarshim* are presented in English. Every quotation is referenced so that the reader can consult the sources in their original — and is encouraged to do so.

Transliterations

- The *ma'amarim* of *Peshuto Shel Mikra* are not introductory level discussions. They presume a basic level of knowledge, both of Torah ideas and of Hebrew terms. For example, words and phrases such as "*Chet Ha'Egel,*" "*ketoret,*" and "*kedushah*" will appear in transliterated form, as opposed to "the sin of the Golden Calf," "incense," and "holiness." As a general guideline, a word for which Rav Copperman himself would use the Hebrew while speaking in English is presented as such in transliterated form.

- Terms that are considered to be beyond introductory in nature will be accompanied by a brief explanatory footnote.
- In transliteration, we used the Sephardi pronunciation, which was the one Rav Copperman used in his *shiurim*.
- For the most part, for the sake of smoother reading we used transliterated English as opposed to Hebrew, with the exception of certain cases where it was judged easier to use the Hebrew words themselves.

Footnotes

- Regular footnotes are the words of Rav Copperman.
- Footnotes in square parentheses are the translator's.

I would like to express my thanks to Dr. Devorah Rosenwasser for initiating and overseeing this project. Her encouragement and enthusiasm were driving forces that kept things moving forward.

I would also like to thank Rav Chaim Pollock and Dr. Debbie Lifshitz who consistently took time from their busy schedules and made themselves available to answer all of my questions concerning style, content, accuracy, and readability, from the most general matters to the most particular.

Lastly, I would like to express my thanks to Rav Mordechai Copperman who allowed me to draw on his fluency and mastery of the teachings of his father, *zt"l*, in *peshuto shel mikra* and met with me on numerous occasions to discuss and elucidate certain difficult passages in the *sefer*.

Translating Rav Copperman's discussions on *peshuto shel mikra* has been a profound learning experience. *Baruch Hashem,* in addition to having a very close family connection with the Rav I had the privilege of learning *b'chavrusa* with him for many years, over the course of which I heard many of the basic *yesodot* numerous times. Nonetheless, to systematically work through the *sefer* and be exposed to the depth and breadth of these discussions was a journey of Torah discovery that opened the eyes, challenged the mind, and gladdened the soul. The only note of sadness that tinged this experience was the knowledge that if I encountered something in the *sefer* that was not clear, I could no longer call Rav Copperman himself to clarify the issue, as I had done on so many previous occasions. It is my hope that this presentation will in some way do justice to his unique and important Torah lessons.

I.B.
Yerushalayim, 5777

INTRODUCTION

Peshuto Shel Mikra

AMONG THE MANY literary Torah achievements of HaRav Yehuda Copperman, *zt"l*, without question the most significant is his monumental *sefer Peshuto Shel Mikra*. This work sets about trying to establish the parameters of *pshat*, as well as its overall role and contribution within the totality of Torah. The fact that such a foundational work waited so long before being written is a tribute to the unique way in which the Rav[1] learned and thought. He learned through virtually the entire corpus of classic *mefarshim* on the Torah, as perhaps others have done as well. Yet where others found *peirushim*, the Rav uncovered principles. While some may have seen before them a body of Torah knowledge, he perceived Torah pathways. For at the same time as he was learning, he was also observing; and when he had finished going through a *devar Torah* he asked himself not only, "What was said here?" but also, "What has this taught me about the methodology of learning Torah or about the way the Torah expresses itself?" With his formidably acute and erudite mind,

---

1   [Those who knew Rav Copperman will no doubt remember that he prided himself on the fact that Michlalah was the only Torah institution in the world where one could not use the term "the Rav" without having to explain to whom one was referring. It is appropriately ironic that as far as many of the students were concerned, *he* was the Rav! Certainly within the context of his *sefer* we have deemed it appropriate to refer to him with this term.]

once he had identified a certain *yesod* in one place, he would "open a file" for that *yesod*, keeping it in mind and taking note of other examples that might corroborate and develop it. The result of this decades-long endeavor is a four-volume work entitled "על מקומו של פשוטו של מקרא בשלימות התורה ובקדושתה — *The Place of Peshuto Shel Mikra within the Totality and Sanctity of the Torah*."

To provide some historical context, the Rav was witness to a situation in which he assessed that the concept of *peshuto shel mikra* — specifically in relation to Midrash Chazal — was the victim of severe injustice. This injustice emanated from two entirely different directions. One the one hand, the only place where *peshuto shel mikra* was being actively studied as a discipline was in academic institutions such as universities. However, there it was treated as the only legitimate way of approaching the words of the *Chumash*, with the *derashot* of Chazal being completely rejected. On the other hand, in the *yeshivot*, it was *peshuto shel mikra* that was sidelined as an area of study, with exclusive emphasis being given to how Chazal interpret the *pesukim* through *midrash halachah*. The Rav saw a dire need for restoring the area of Torah study known as *peshuto shel mikra* to its rightful place within the *shleimut* of Torah, not in competition with the *drash*, but working alongside it.

Ain Mikra Yotzei Midei Peshuto

One of the most important statements of Chazal regarding the concept of *pshat*, and to which the Rav devoted a great deal of attention, is their assertion that "אֵין מִקְרָא יוֹצֵא מִידֵי פְּשׁוּטוֹ — *the pasuk never departs from its pshat*" (*Shabbat* 63a; *Yevamot* 24a). One of the things the Rav emphasized regularly regarding this statement is that it was made by Chazal *themselves*, whose primary area of involvement was that of *midrash halachah*! *They* were the ones who stressed that the *pasuk* does not depart from its *pshat*. The Rav identified two primary approaches among the *mefarshim* as to how to understand this statement. Ultimately, he categorized the proponents of each approach into two distinct "*batei midrash*," in his words.

The first approach explains that although initially it may seem as if the *pshat* of the *pasuk* is at odds with the halachah as we know it, upon further and more rigorous analysis of the *pasuk* we will discover that the *pshat* is actually compatible with the halachah. This means that the *halachic* interpretation never constitutes a complete departure from *peshuto shel mikra*. Classic proponents of this approach are the *Malbim* and the *HaKetav VeHakabbalah*.

The second approach was the one with which the Rav himself identified, and which essentially formed the basis of his discussions of *peshuto shel mikra*. This understanding states that while the halachah may be derived from the *pasuk*,[2] it is not at all the product of the area known as *pshat*, but rather of a different methodology — *drash*. The *pshat* itself remains distinct from the halachah. That said, Chazal are telling us that even if the *pshat* does not teach us the halachah, nonetheless it does have a message that it is crucial to our full understanding of the matter at hand.

According to this approach, for example, when the Torah says that the punishment for putting someone's eye out is "עַיִן תַּחַת עָיִן — *an eye for an eye*," although we know that the halachah is that the damager pays the monetary value of the victim's eye, we are not to understand that the actual *pshat* of the *pasuk* is really referring to money. Rather, the *pshat* is that he should lose his eye. Once the halachah states that this does not happen literally, we then need to ask, why did the Torah write the *pasuk* in a way that the *pshat* tells me that he loses an eye if in practice this will not happen? Among the classic proponents of this second approach, and from whom the Rav quotes numerous times throughout the *sefer*, are the Vilna Gaon and the *Meshech Chochmah*.

She'eylat HaKeytzad and She'eylat HaMadua

Understanding the relationship between *pshat* and *drash* will mean that whenever the halachah differs from the *pshat* of the *pasuk*, there are two questions we will need to ask.

---

2   [In his terminology, "בנוי על הכתוב," built, or based, upon the *pasuk*.]

1. *Keytzad* — How? How in fact do we know that the halachah is not as the *pshat* would seem to indicate? How do we know that "*ayin tachat ayin*" in practice means monetary payment and not the loss of an eye? How do we know that when the Torah says that we should begin counting the *Omer* "*mimacharat haShabbat*" this is telling us to begin counting on the second day of Pesach and not specifically on Sunday? The answer to this question will typically lie in the area of *midrash halachah*. In the Gemara, answering this first question of "*keytzad*" is the primary goal of the *sugya's* treatment of the *pasuk*.

2. *Madua* — Why? Having established that the halachah differs from the *pshat*, we then proceed to ask the following question: *why* did the Torah write the *pasuk* in such a way that the *pshat* does not reflect the halachah? If the damager pays money, why did the Torah write that he should lose his eye? If the *Omer* is counted from the second day of Pesach, why did the Torah refer to it as "*mimacharat haShabbat*"? It is the answer to this second question of "*madua*" that will help us uncover the role of *pshat* within the Torah's message in every area.[3]

Peshuto Shel Mikra is thus not a *sefer* like other *sefarim* on the *Chumash*. It is expressly focused on the foundations and concepts related to *pshat*. It contains hundreds of *peirushim*, but they are presented and examined primarily in terms of the light they shed on *peshuto shel mikra*. In the Rav's words, awareness of the function of *pshat* within Torah means that it is not sufficient to ask the question, "מה הפשט — what is the *pshat*?" Rather, one must follow up with the question, "מה הפשט מלמד — what does the *pshat* **teach**?" How does it make its unique contribution within the full picture of what the Torah wants to teach me?

---

3   [These two questions will form the basis of the first two *ma'amarim* of this *choveret*.]

One of the remarkable things about this *sefer* is that it contains many *yesodot* that one could be considered quite learned without knowing, and yet they are so fundamental that after learning them one asks, "How could I have learned *Chumash* and not known that?" There is no question that learning the concepts and principles in the Rav's *sefer* will bring about a tangible and quantifiable increase in both the depth and scope of one's Torah knowledge.

Kedushat Peshuto Shel Mikra

The original *sefer Peshuto Shel Mikra* is a formidable work, with lengthy discussions, a deluge of sources enlisted to develop the topic, and copious amounts of footnotes. Indeed, the Rav himself discerned that this was not a *sefer* for everyone, and he therefore created a simplified version that he called *Kedushat Peshuto Shel Mikra*. This new *sefer* is not arranged according to topic, but instead is based on the *Parashat Hashavua*. Each *parashah* contains a number of *ma'amarim*, with the point of departure being a *pasuk* in that *parashah* that relates to a certain aspect of *peshuto shel mikra*. The chapters are shorter, designed to give a most basic introduction to that particular idea, almost like a taster, and are generally intended to make these *yesodot* more accessible and understandable to the broader public.

The Rav's Literary Style

In both the original *Peshuto Shel Mikra* as well as in *Kedushat Peshuto*, the Rav displayed a writing style that is quite unique. In terms of language, he blended Rabbinic idioms and high-level modern Hebrew into an integrated and harmonized medium. This is one of the aspects that might present a challenge to a reader who is versed in the one but not in the other.

In terms of presentation as well, his *sefarim* were unique. His discourse is always clear, but never rigid. His ideas are always high-level and can often get quite involved, yet are also presented with disarming informality. I believe one of the reasons for this is that the Rav saw himself first and foremost as "מורה בישראל," a teacher in Yisrael, and as such, even as he produced many *sefarim*, he was not so much "writing a *sefer*," but rather "teaching in writing," with the reader becoming his student. The goal was thus effective and engaging communication instead of creating a literary work per se. Thus, he will often add in parenthetical comments and occasionally digress to a related matter, as a teacher would, in order to create a fuller discussion and ensure that the reader has not lost sight of certain key points that are crucial for a true understanding of the topic under discussion.

Peshuto Shel Mikra in English

It is a great *zechut* to be able to present some of the Rav's Torah to the English-speaking community. Although the Rav himself almost never wrote in English, he was very encouraging of the idea and gave his heartfelt *berachah* to it. While we would have loved for him to have seen the results of this project, we at least hope that it will be a source of *nachat* for him. *Baruch Hashem*, translation of the *sefer Kedushat Peshuto Shel Mikra* into English is underway, and the contents of this *choveret* are a selection of *ma'amarim* that have been translated so far.

About This *Choveret*

In this pilot work, we have tried to present examples of three key areas that comprise the *sefer* itself:

1. **Functions of *Pshat*** — As mentioned above, once we have established that, in many instances, the *pshat* and the halachah are not the same, the following question then arises: if the *pshat* is not teaching me the halachah, what, then, *is* it teaching me? In the *sefer Peshuto Shel Mikra*, The Rav identified no less than eleven distinct functions of *pshat*, that is, different ways that *pshat* makes its contribution to the full message the Torah wants to tell us. As the Rav used

to say, "The *pshat* may not always teach the halachah, but it always teaches Torah!"

2. **Signon HaKatuv** — The Rav paid particular attention to the different ways or styles (*signon*) in which the Torah expresses itself, and discussed the differences between these different styles. For example, sometimes the Torah commands that something *should* happen, while other times it describes something that *will* happen. While both are the words of the Torah, they convey different types of messages and may not necessarily obligate equally on a halachic level. Similarly, sometimes the Torah quotes someone as speaking. Whose words are these: the person's or the Torah's? If we conclude that they are "the Torah's presentation of the person's words," is there a difference between words that the Torah "itself" says and those that it quotes someone as saying? It is important to note, as the Rav demonstrates, that sensitivity to *signon hakatuv* and the way something is presented in the Torah will have implications both for the halachic and the non-halachic sections.

3. **General Concepts** — In the course of his extensive investigations into *pshat* and related matters, many broader principles pertaining to how to understand *Chumash* were also developed. Does the location where a certain mitzvah is written in the Torah make a difference to our understanding of that mitzvah? Why does the Torah sometimes present aspects of a specific mitzvah in two or more different places? How many different types of explanations of Chazal are there? Is it possible for a mitzvah to belong to more than one category of mitzvot?

It is our hope that these selected *ma'amarim* will reflect not only the critical importance and value of the Rav's discussions, but also the joy and excitement with which he would transmit them. For, as anyone who had the *zechut* of being taught by him will no doubt remember, his joy in sharing words of Torah was boundless, and it was contagious.

We look forward with Hashem's help to making the entire *sefer* available in the not-too-distant future. Until then, may these words be an *ilui l'neshmah* for our beloved and unforgettable Rav Copperman, and may his message continue to spread through the spoken and written word —

עד ביאת הגואל, אמן

FUNCTIONS OF

PSHAT

Section A

Ma'amar One

PSHAT REFLECTS WHAT SHOULD HAPPEN ON A D'ORAITA LEVEL – AYIN TACHAT AYIN

She'eylat HaKeytzad — Asking "How"

THE TORAH STATES that the punishment for inflicting injury on another is "עַיִן תַּחַת עַיִן — *an eye for an eye*" (*Shemot* 21:24). As we know, the halachah is that the perpetrator does not actually have his own eye taken out but instead pays the victim the value of his eye. Ramban (*Peirush* to *Shemot* ibid.) explains that this is based on a tradition received by Chazal ("*Kabbalat Rabboteinu*").[4] Similarly, the Rambam writes, "This is how our fathers saw the *din* being conducted in the *beit din* of Yehoshua and in the *beit din* of Shmuel Haramati, and in every *beit din* that existed from the days of Moshe Rabbeinu until now" (*Hilchot Chovel U'Mazik* 1:6).

---

4   [We should emphasize — as the Rav himself did — that the use of the word "*kabbalah*" here refers to a tradition that was received by Chazal regarding a certain Torah matter and not to the area of *nistar* — the hidden parts of the Torah — as the word is commonly used elsewhere.]

At the same time, the Gemara (*Bava Kama* 83b–84a) Did not refrain from getting involved in the question of *"keytzad,"* namely, how can we find a source for *kabbalat Chazal* in the *pesukim* even though the basis for the halachah is not the *pasuk* but the *kabbalah* of Chazal? After a long discussion (two *amudim* of Gemara!), Chazal find a source for the halachah through a *gezeirah shavah*.[5]

She'eylat HaMadua — Asking "Why"

At this stage we proceed to ask the question of *"madua"*? Why did the Torah not simply write, "He shall pay *the value* of the eye," which would thereby teach us the halachah in a way that is clear and leaves no room for misunderstanding? What do we gain from the Torah's writing the penalty in a way that the *pshat* understanding differs from the halachah?

The *Seforno* answers (s.v. *ayin*):

> *This is what **should** have happened based on "hadin hag-amur" (absolute justice),[6] for this is middah k'neged middah. Except that **the kabbalah** of Chazal then tells us that he pays the monetary value, due to our inability to execute the punishment precisely, for perhaps we may make a mistake and inflict undue injury (on the perpetrator) for which we would then be culpable.*

In other words, according to the *Seforno*, the *pshat* of *"ayin tachat ayin"* does not teach us halachah. That is taught by *kabbalat Chazal*.

---

5   *Gezeirah shavah* is one of the principles of *midrash halachah* whereby a key word that features in two different places in Torah allows us to learn *halachot* from one to the other. In this instance, the halachah certainly preceded the *drash*. In the *sefer Peshuto Shel Mikra* (section 1, chapter 9) we discussed at length the *machloket* between the Netziv and the *Ohr HaChaim* regarding the benefit of establishing a basis for a received halachah through the principles of *midrash halachah*.

6   This is in keeping with the view of the *Seforno* that the *pesukim* in *Parashat Mishpatim*, prior to the *Chet Ha'Egel*, represent the maximum level of absolute justice from which we fell as a result of the *Chet Ha'Egel*.

What it does teach us are two things:

1. How the halachah would look were Am Yisrael to be operating on a level of absolute justice. Operating on that level
would create a risk of killing the perpetrator while trying to
just take out his eye. We should note that this explanation
offered by the *Seforno* is actually one of the proofs that
Chazal themselves (*Bava Kama* ibid.) sought to bring for the
interpretation of "*mamon,*" but they subsequently rejected it.
This rejected proof was then "resurrected" by the *Seforno,* so
that his words are ultimately sourced in Chazal, just not in
their conclusion![7]

2. A *mussar* (ethical) statement that teaches the perpetrator
a crucial lesson in how the Torah looks at these matters. A
person shouldn't think that in the same way that if he breaks
someone's window the punishment is two hundred dollars,
so too if he puts his eye out the punishment is two thousand
dollars, so that the difference between them is simply the
amount of money paid. Rather, the Torah teaches us through
peshuto shel mikra: "Know that you really deserve to have
your eye taken out just as you took his out, exactly like נֶפֶשׁ
תַּחַת נָפֶשׁ — *a soul for a soul.* In that case no one asks, what does
the family of the dead person gain from the *beit din* killing
his murderer, for it is *middah k'neged middah.*" So too here,
based on *middah k'neged middah,* the punishment should
be "*ayin tachat ayin*" — *mamash!* In contrast, had the Torah
written "*d'mei eino yeshalem* — he shall pay the value of his
eye," it would have thereby equated the value of a person's
limbs with that of the rest of his property.

We see here how the *pshat* functions as an integral part of
kedushat haTorah, albeit not on a halachic plane, and teaches us

---

7 This phenomenon, which is quite prevalent among the *mefarshim,* is discussed in
our *peirush* to the *Seforno, Shemot* 21:24.

what should have been the verdict based on *"hadin hagamur,"* whereas the midrash teaches us the actual halachah. And this is most fitting, for the *shleimut haTorah* is expressed through each method of learning, which gives us an additional aspect of that totality.

"Ayin Tachat Ayin" K'peshuto Affecting the Halachah

However, after examining the words of *"HaNesher Hagadol"* — the **Rambam** — it seems that *"ayin tachat ayin"* on a *pshat* level actually *does* function in the halachic sphere. Before we discuss the halachah that the Rambam derived from *peshuto shel mikra*, let us first direct our attention to his words (*Hilchot Chovel U'Mazik* 1:3) that are similar in approach to those of the *Seforno* but phrased in the unique style of the Rambam:

> *That which the Torah states (Vayikra 24:20), "Just as he inflicted a wound on a person, so shall it be inflicted upon him," does not mean that we should injure him just like he injured the other person. Rather, it means he is **deserving** of losing a limb or suffering injury as he himself inflicted. And therefore he pays for the injury. Behold, the pasuk states (Bamidbar 35:31),* "וְלֹא תִקְחוּ כֹפֶר לְנֶפֶשׁ רֹצֵחַ" *— do not take ransom for the soul of the murderer," [this teaches us that] only for a murderer we do not take ransom,[8] but for loss of a limb or other injury there is ransom.*

Looking at these words, we cannot help but ask ourselves, why is the Rambam in the *Mishneh Torah* getting involved in *parshanut* of the Torah? If the Rambam states that "he is deserving of losing a limb," what are the halachic implications that he is looking to glean from *peshuto shel mikra*? After all, the Rambam's *Mishneh Torah* deals with *halachot*, not with *parshanut*!

---

8   [I.e. allow him to offer monetary restitution in lieu of physical punishment.]

The **Rambam** himself provides the answer (*Hilchot Chovel U'Mazik* 5:9):

> *Damaging a person bodily is not the same as damaging his property. If one damages his fellow's property, once he has paid him what he is obligated to pay he has received kaparah. However, if one injures his fellow, even if he has paid him all five payments he has not received kaparah. Even if one were to offer all eilei nevayot[9] as korbanot he would not receive kaparah, nor would his sin be forgiven until he asks the injured person for forgiveness.*

Here we see an explicit halachah being learned from *peshuto shel mikra*! The law of one who injures his fellow is not the same as one who damages his property. When he inflicts injury, he is "deserving of losing a limb," and this concept finds expression in a **practical obligation** (to ask for forgiveness), for it withholds from him the *kaparah* that he would otherwise receive. Thus, the idea of "he is deserving" derived from *peshuto shel mikra* translates into *hilchot teshuvah d'Oraita*! Had it said "*demei eino yeshalem*," his status would be the same as if he damaged his fellow's property, both in *beit din shel matah* and in *beit din shel Maalah*.[10]

Further Implications

Elsewhere, too, it seems that **Rambam** has understood "*ayin tachat ayin*" *k'peshuto* as functioning in the halachic sphere (*Hilchot Chovel U'Mazik* 4:9):

> *If one injures his fellow on Yom Kippur, even intentionally,[11] he is liable to pay [all five payments for injury], even though*

---

9   [A phrase used by Chazal (*Bava Kama* 92a) to imply a multitude of animals, based on *Yeshaya* 60:7.]

10   See also Rambam *Hilchot Teshuvah* 2:9.

11   Since this act would incur the punishment of *karet*, not death through *beit din,* it would make the person liable for *malkot* (see next footnote).

he committed an aveirah that makes him liable to receive malkot,[12] *and the general rule is that "one who is liable for both malkot and monetary payment receives malkot and does not pay,"*[13] *for one does not both receive malkot and a monetary penalty. That is generally true in all such cases, with the exception of physical injury, for the Torah explicitly included one who injures his fellow in monetary payments, as it says, "*רַק שִׁבְתּוֹ יִתֵּן וְרַפֹּא יְרַפֵּא*" — only for his lost time he shall pay, and for his healing" (Shemot 21:19).*

We would like to suggest that behind the source in the *pasuk* (*gezeirat hakatuv*), which the Rambam provided to explain the ruling of "receiving *malkot* and having to pay," lies the principle of "*ayin tachat ayin*" — *k'peshuto mamash*! Let us explain as follows. The *d'Oraita* rule of "*risha'a achat*," only incurring one penalty, only applies with regards to two different **types** of penalty, such as *malkot* and monetary payment. It is clear, however, that if one did an action that made him liable for two or three sets of *malkot* [for example, plowing with an ox and donkey together on Yom Kippur during the *Shemittah* year], he would receive *malkot* for each separate *aveirah*.

Therefore, had the Torah written "*demei eino yeshalem*," we would apply the restricting rule of "*kidei rishato*," for then we would be dealing with two different types of punishment: bodily punishment for violating Yom Kippur, and monetary punishment for injuring his fellow. However, once the Torah writes "*ayin tachat ayin*," we are now dealing with **two bodily punishments** (his eye and *malkot*), and therefore he is liable for both of them!

According to this understanding, it turns out that "*ayin tachat ayin*" is **k'peshuto** (i.e., "*mamash*") with regards to the **essence** of the *din*, but becomes **monetary** when it comes to its **implementation**.

---

12   Since all *aveirot* that incur *karet* can incur *malkot* if he is warned by witnesses (*Ketuvot* 32a).

13   As discussed in Gemara *Makkot* 13b based on the words "כְּדֵי רִשְׁעָתוֹ — *kidei rishato*," we make him liable for one penalty and not for two.

It was this monetary execution that was witnessed in every *beit din*, from the *beit din* of Yehoshua down to the *beit din* of the Rambam. This appears to us to be the explanation of the idea that "injuring one's fellow is not the same as damaging his property."

R' Eliezer's View

This idea will perhaps give us a deeper understanding of the position of R' Eliezer (*Bava Kama* 84a) who states that "*ayin tachat ayin*" means *mamash* — literally! The Gemara explains that R' Eliezer holds that the amount paid is not the value of the victim's eye, but rather that of the one who injured him. All agree that the practical implementation of this *din* is in the form of monetary payment; no one ever imagined that it would be otherwise. However, R' Eliezer, who is from the *beit midrash* of Shamai HaZaken, paves the way for the *Seforno*'s understanding that the *pasuk* is referring to absolute justice, "*hadin hagamur*" — and who will expect absolute justice if not the *beit midrash* of Shamai HaZaken! If indeed absolute justice demands *middah k'neged middah*, then the monetary payment must be the value of the **damager's eye** — for it is his eye that should have been taken out — and not the value of the victim's eye. This is very clearly "ransom" for the damager's eye and not "payment" for the victim's eye.

With this we can understand with full precision the words of the *pasuk* in the case of a murderer (*Bamidbar* 35:31), "וְלֹא תִקְחוּ כֹפֶר לְנֶפֶשׁ רֹצֵחַ — *do not take ransom for the soul of the murderer*," from which Chazal infer (*Bava Kama* 83b), "אבל לראשי אברים אתה לוקח — *but for loss of limb you may take ransom*." According to R' Eliezer, we are taking ransom of the damager's eye that should have been taken out, as opposed to the case of murder where we take his soul *mamash*, with no possibility of ransom.

Ma'amar Two

PSHAT TEACHES THE NATURE
OR ESSENCE OF THE MITZVAH –
MIMACHARAT HASHABBAT

וּסְפַרְתֶּם לָכֶם מִמָּחֳרַת הַשַּׁבָּת

You shall count for yourselves from the morrow
of the Shabbat (Vayikra 23:15).

TWO FUNDAMENTAL QUESTIONS occupy the mind
of one who learns *Torah SheBichtav* and *Torah SheBaal Peh al taharat
hakodesh*:

1. *She'eylat HaKeytzad* — Asking "**how**." *How* do Chazal know
   to explain the *pasuk* in the way that they do, when their
   explanation seems to differ from the *pshat* of the *pasuk*?
   For example, as we discussed above, that *"ayin tachat ayin"*
   means monetary compensation?
2. *She'eylat HaMadua* — Asking "**why**." Once we have succeeded
   in understanding the *peirush* of Chazal (bearing in mind the
   words of the Netziv, that "Anyone who explains the *pshat* in
   accordance with his own understanding, without first having

understood the approach of Chazal to that *pasuk*, there is room to suspect him of *akiporsut*, explaining the *pesukim* in accordance with their [the *Apikorsim's*] approach"), we turn to the second question, which is asking *why* did Hashem tell Moshe Rabbeinu to write the *pasuk* in a way where the simple meaning of the words does not seem to fit in with the halachah as derived by Chazal? This is especially troubling when we realize that it was Chazal themselves who stated that "אֵין מִקְרָא יוֹצֵא מִידֵי פְּשׁוּטוֹ — *the pasuk never departs from its straightforward (pshat) interpretation*" (*Yevamot* 24a).[14] In other words, we are asking, what does the *pshat* teach us in addition to what we learned from the midrash, all of this within the *shleimut* of the Torah?

Refuting the Baytusim, Kara'im, and Maskilim

When it comes to the *sugya* of "*Mimacharat HaShabbat*," the difficulty lies not only with the question of "*madua*," but also with the question of "*keytzad.*" How do we know that the term "*mimacharat haShabbat*" refers not to Sunday, but to the second day of Pesach? Chazal dealt with the question of "*keytzad*" over the course of three entire *amudim* of Gemara in *Masechet Menachot* (65a–66a) and presented several solutions. At the end of this long discussion, Chazal themselves concluded that all of these explanations have a difficulty, with the exception of the final two suggestions of the *Tanna'im*. In other words, only two of the five resolutions mentioned are considered effective. We should also mention that the two resolutions that are accepted by Chazal are not based on principles of *pshat* so that they wouldn't actually present an approach that would satisfy the Baytusim (Boethusians), with whom Chazal were debating. The Baytusim only accepted explanations that were based on *pshat* principles that they recognized as legitimate, and, according to *peshuto*

---

14   This subject has been discussed at length in the two introductory chapters of *Peshuto Shel Mikra*.

shel mikra, the words "*mimacharat haShabbat*" refer to the first day of the week — Sunday! If so, the question returns, why did Hashem dictate to Moshe the words "*mimacharat haShabbat*" and then explain to us that the reference is to the second day of Pesach?

In fact, historically, the matter went further. This approach of the Baytusim of understanding the Torah based exclusively on *peshuto shel mikra* was revived in the time of the *Ge'onim* in the form of the Kara'im (Karaites), which then led to further refutations of their *peirush* by R' Saadia Gaon, Ibn Ezra, and others, and once again in the period of the Maskilim, this time with additional refutations coming from *HaKetav VeHakabbalah*, the *Malbim*, R' David Tzvi Hoffman, and others. All of this seems to indicate that the answer to the question of "*keytzad*" is not clear, for, if the original resolutions were fully successful in demonstrating how "*mimacharat haShabbat*" on the level of *pshat* really means "*mimacharat haPesach*," the question would not keep on coming back again and again. Moreover, there would be no need to produce new resolutions of this question that had not been considered by the earlier *mefarshim*. In any event, these discussions represent an approach that seeks to prove to the other side (Baytusim, Kara'im, Maskilim) that the *derashah* or *kabbalah* of Chazal is actually in line with *peshuto shel mikra*, since according to their opinion this is the only legitimate way of understanding the words of the Torah.

The *Meshech Chochmah's* Approach

For our part, we have no need to defend the *kabbalah* of Chazal — received from Moshe Rabbeinu, down the generations through Chazal, *Rishonim*, and *Acharonim* — that the authentic halachic explanation of the word "Shabbat" in the *pasuk* is that it refers to the first day of Pesach. Nevertheless, as people learning Torah *al taharat hakodesh*, there is certainly room to ask the question "*madua?*" There is no doubt that the *pshat*-meaning of the word "Shabbat" — which appears countless times in Tanach — refers to the seventh day of the week. If so, **why** did the Torah choose to refer to the calendar date of the fifteenth of Nissan as "Shabbat"?

In an attempt to answer the question of "*madua*," we will follow the path of **R' Meir Simcha HaKohen of Dvinsk** in his *peirush Meshech Chochmah*, who deals with this problem in numerous places. His basic approach is to identify certain characteristics that both Pesach and Shabbat have in common so that it becomes possible to understand why one would be called by the name of the other. Let us begin by referring to two places where the *Meshech Chochmah* points out similarities between Pesach and Shabbat in the realm of *machshavah*.

The First Approach — Days That Connect Us to Hashem and Days That Connect Us to Each Other

In his *peirush* to *Parashat Emor* (23:21, s.v. *chukat olam*),[15] the *Meshech Chochmah* divides the mitzvot of the Torah into two categories:

A. Mitzvot that connect Yisrael to Hashem (e.g., *tzitzit*, *tefillin*, *mezuzah*).
B. Mitzvot that connect Yisrael to each other (e.g. *gemilut chassadim*).

This distinction between these different types of mitzvot finds expression in the difference between the day of Shabbat on the one hand, when all *melachah* is forbidden, including cooking and carrying, so that the emphasis is on connecting Am Yisrael with Hashem, and the *Mo'adim* on the other hand, when carrying and cooking are permitted, so that Am Yisrael can connect more with each other. With regards to this distinction, we can see that in a number of ways Pesach is more similar to Shabbat than it is to the other *Mo'adim*:

1. One needs to be registered (*manui*) with a *korban pesach* on Erev Pesach, and no provisions can be made once Pesach has

---

15   This section of *Meshech Chochmah* is quite lengthy; therefore, we have chosen to present a digest of his explanation in our own words. The reader is invited to consult his words in the original and may find our commentary there to be of assistance.

arrived. This is similar to what we find in regard to Shabbat, where the Gemara (*Avodah Zarah* 3a) tells us, "Whoever prepares on *Erev Shabbat* shall eat on Shabbat."

2. On the original Pesach in Mitzrayim, Bnei Yisrael were told (*Shemot* 12:22), "וְאַתֶּם לֹא תֵצְאוּ אִישׁ מִפֶּתַח בֵּיתוֹ עַד בֹּקֶר" — *and no man from among you shall leave the entrance of his house until morning,*" which corresponds to the commandment of (ibid. 16:29), "אַל יֵצֵא אִישׁ מִמְּקֹמוֹ בַּיּוֹם הַשְּׁבִיעִי" — *let no man leave his place on the seventh day.*"

Therefore, explains the *Meshech Chochmah,* since Pesach is more similar in nature to Shabbat than to the other *Mo'adim* in this key regard, the Torah actually refers to it in our *Parashah* as "Shabbat."

The Second Approach — Active and Passive Relationships between Bnei Yisrael and Hashem

In a second discussion (*Devarim* 5:15, s.v. *ve'zacharta*), the *Meshech Chochmah* deals with the question of how Bnei Yisrael historically came to be connected to Hashem in their formative stages as "Am Hashem." Here, too, he sees remarkable similarities between Shabbat and Pesach on the one hand, and the other *Mo'adim,* specifically Shavuot and Succot, on the other. Shabbat was a day that we received as a "gift" from Hashem, with no prior input on our part. Similarly, we were redeemed from Mitzrayim on Pesach even though we were at that time "עֵרֹם וְעֶרְיָה" — bereft of mitzvot.[16] In contrast, when it comes to Shavuot, we participated in the giving of the Torah by accepting it wholeheartedly with *na'aseh v'nishma.*[17] Similarly, the return of the *Ananei HaKavod* after the *Chet Ha'Egel,* which we commemorate on the *chag* of Succot, came about as a result of our *teshuvah* for the *Chet Ha'Egel.*[18] Thus, the *Mo'adim* of Shavuot and Succot are ones in which we were active participants, whereas Pesach

---

16   *Yechezkel* 16:7, as explained by Chazal.
17   *Shemot* 24:7.
18   [See *peirush* of the *Vilna Gaon* to *Shir HaShirim* 1:4.]

is more like Shabbat in the sense that we were passive recipients, and that is another reason why the Torah calls the first day of Pesach "Shabbat."

The Third Approach — Root Similarities

We come now to the third discussion of the *Meshech Chochmah* (*Shemot* 12:17, s.v. *u'shemartem et hamatzot*). It is worthwhile noting that this is the only place where he explicitly concludes his discussion with the words "*and it is for this reason* that Pesach is referred to as Shabbat," which seems to indicate that he considers this approach to be the one that best answers the question. Here, the *Meshech Chochmah* moves from a *machshavah* or historical discussion to one that discusses **the essence and roots of the mitzvah**.

In this approach, the *Meshech Chochmah* points out that the root שמר, meaning "to guard," or "to keep," appears numerous times in the Torah with regards to Shabbat as well as with regards to Pesach. Since the term שמר has a connotation of a *lo taaseh* — a negative prohibition,[19] it emerges that the dominant element of Shabbat, as well as of Pesach, is that of *lo taaseh*, as opposed to an *aseh* — a positive mitzvah. This has major ramifications for the way in which we are to view the mitzvot of Shabbat, for, instead of seeing its *aseh* and *lo taaseh* as separate mitzvot, we are to view them as being connected, with the *aseh* being **influenced by** the *lo taaseh*. Indeed, as a result of this influence, when we look at the *aseh* it is no longer a "normal" or "pure" *aseh*; rather, it is a "composite mitzvah," that is to say, an *aseh* that contains within it an element of *lo taaseh*, on account of the number of times the Torah mentions "*shamor*" in connection with Shabbat.

Halachic Ramifications

It is for this reason women are obligated in the positive mitzvah of *kiddush* ("*zachor*") even though women are generally exempt from

---

19   [See, for example, *Eiruvin* 96a.]

mitzvot aseh if they are *zman grama* — time bound, such as the mitzvah of tzitzit or of dwelling in a succah.[20] Here, since the dominant element of *lo taaseh* has permeated the *aseh* element, it has removed from it the status of a "pure" *aseh*, and women are thus not exempted from the *aseh* of Shabbat. This is the deeper understanding of what Chazal meant when they said that "זָכוֹר וְשָׁמוֹר בְּדִבּוּר אֶחָד נֶאֶמְרוּ — *'zachor'* and 'shamor' were said simultaneously."* In other words, when it comes to Shabbat, we do not look upon the positive and negative mitzvot as distinct from each other; rather, we look upon them as connected and capable of influencing and affecting each other.

When it comes to Pesach, we find the exact same thing. There, too, the Torah uses the term שמר many times, reflecting the negative element. For example, the Torah says (*Shemot* 12:17), "וּשְׁמַרְתֶּם אֶת הַמַּצּוֹת — *you shall guard the matzot (from becoming chametz)*," and not 'וַאֲפִיתֶם אֶת הַמַּצּוֹת — *you shall **bake** the matzot.*' Thus, we find that women are obligated in the positive mitzvah of eating matzah on Pesach. Even though this too is *zman grama*, from which women are generally exempt, nevertheless, there is something about this mitzvah that makes it an exception to the rule.

This is the underlying basis for the *derashah* of Chazal on the *pasuk,* which links the mitzvah of eating matzah with not eating chametz, "לֹא תֹאכַל עָלָיו חָמֵץ שִׁבְעַת יָמִים תֹּאכַל עָלָיו מַצּוֹת" (*Devarim* 16:3). The Gemara (*Pesachim* 43b) explains, "This teaches us that whoever is included in the *issur* of eating chametz is included in the mitzvah of eating matzah. From here R' Eliezer said that women are obligated in the mitzvah of eating matzah on a *d'Oraita* level." Or, to put it differently, the relationship between not eating chametz and eating matzah is not simply a halachic equation (*hekesh*) between two mitzvot based on *semichut* (juxtaposition). Rather, it is revealing that, on a root level, the positive mitzvah of matzah is influenced by the dominant *lo taaseh* element (due to the extensive use of the word שמר) so that it has lost its status as a "pure" *mitzvat aseh* and hence is

---

20   [See *Masechet Berachot* 20b.]

no longer part of the general rule regarding *mitzvot aseh she'hazman grama* from which women are exempt.[21]

This is a truly remarkable *chiddush* of the *Meshech Chochmah* in the *sugya* of "composite mitzvot in the Torah" and the way it can shape the *halachot* of those mitzvot, a *chiddush* worthy of the great *gaon*, R' Meir Simcha HaKohen of Dvinsk.

It is on the basis of this similarity between the makeup of the mitzvot of Pesach and Shabbat that R' Meir Simcha understands why the Torah calls Pesach "Shabbat." This is the expression in *peshuto shel mikra* regarding the essential nature of Pesach. It is not just another *Mo'ed* within the various *Mo'adim*; rather, it belongs in great measure to the "family" of Shabbat, so that we could really refer to it as "a *Shabbosdik* Yom Tov"!

Pesach throughout the *Chumashim*

Based on this idea, let us follow the *Mo'ed* of Pesach through the various *Chumashim*, and we will see that it began (in *Chumash Shemot*) with the status of Shabbat, moved on (in *Chumash Vayikra*) to the category of (pure) Yom Tov, and finally (in *Chumash Devarim*) returned in some measure to its original status as Shabbat.

Chumash Shemot — The first time the Torah presents the mitzvot of Pesach, it writes (*Shemot* 12:16), "וּבַיּוֹם הָרִאשׁוֹן מִקְרָא קֹדֶשׁ וּבַיּוֹם הַשְּׁבִיעִי מִקְרָא קֹדֶשׁ יִהְיֶה לָכֶם כָּל מְלָאכָה לֹא יֵעָשֶׂה בָהֶם — *on the first day it shall be a holy calling, and on the seventh day it shall be for you a holy calling, **no***

---

21   Based on this approach, the *Meshech Chochmah* suggests an answer to a question of *Tosafot* in *Yevamot* (4a) where the Gemara identifies a *hekesh* between the mitzvot of not wearing *shaatnez* and making tzitzit. *Tosafot* ask, why are women not obligated in the mitzvah of tzitzit? Surely we should say, "whoever is included in the *issur* of *shaatnez* is included in the mitzvah of tzitzit" in the same way that we said regarding *chametz* and matzah! According to the *Meshech Chochmah*, the way Chazal learned that women are obligated in kiddush on Shabbat and matzah on Pesach is not based on a *hekesh* and juxtaposition alone. Rather, it was through the understanding that Shabbat and Pesach each really contain a composite mitzvah, with the negative (שמר) element being dominant, so that the positive element is not part of the general rule to exempt women. *Shaatnez* and tzitzit have no such relationship to each other, and therefore there is no reason not to exempt women from the time-bound mitzvah of tzitzit.

melachah may be performed on them." Here, Pesach is presented in the same way as Shabbat, namely, with a prohibition against **any** *melachah*. This is why the *pasuk* immediately qualifies this seeming total equation with Shabbat and continues, "אַךְ אֲשֶׁר יֵאָכֵל לְכָל נֶפֶשׁ הוּא לְבַדּוֹ יֵעָשֶׂה לָכֶם — *only that which is eaten by any person, that alone may be done for you."*

The way the Torah prohibits *melachah* on Shabbat is with the words *"kol melachah,"* whereas for Yom Tov it says (*Vayikra* 23:7), "כָּל מְלֶאכֶת עֲבֹדָה לֹא תַעֲשׂוּ — *do not perform* **melechet avodah**." The Ramban there explains that the term *"melechet avodah"* includes any *melachah* that is not connected to cooking and the like, for those are termed *"melechet hana'ah — melachot* of enjoyment." If so, then the Torah should have also written in *Shemot* regarding Pesach not to do *"melechet avodah"* and would have "saved itself the trouble" of first prohibiting all *melachah* and then having to go back and permit *melachot* that are connected to preparing food! However, had the Torah written it that way, then it would have been presenting Pesach as being entirely similar to all other *Mo'adim*, which it is not! Therefore, by first prohibiting "all *melachah*" and only then qualifying "except [*melachah* done to prepare food]," the Torah is presenting Pesach as "Shabbat minus," as opposed to the other *Yamim Tovim*. In *Sefer Shemot* the Torah provides a **heter** for *melachot* involved in preparing food, whereas in *Chumash Vayikra* that type of *melachah* was **never restricted** in the first place, for it is *melechet hana'ah!*

Chumash Vayikra — The "transition" of the prohibition of *melachah* on Pesach from *"kol melachah"* to *"melechet avodah"* takes place in *Chumash Vayikra* (quoted above). There, it takes leave of its initial "similar to Shabbat" status and joins the other *Mo'adim*, so that *"melechet hana'ah"* of preparing food is naturally permitted.

Chumash Devarim — However, the "*Shabbosdik*" nature of Pesach does not completely disappear, for, in *Chumash Devarim* (16:8), we find that the Torah says in regards to Pesach, "וּבַיּוֹם הַשְּׁבִיעִי עֲצֶרֶת לַה' אֱלֹהֶיךָ לֹא תַעֲשֶׂה מְלָאכָה — *and on the seventh day it shall be an assembly before Hashem your God, do not perform* **melachah**"! The *mefarshim* there struggle to explain what is behind this unique expression of "*melachah*," which is not exactly "*kol melachah*" (appropriate for Shabbat), but neither is it "*melechet avodah*" (appropriate for a Mo'ed). It is just "*melachah*," which seems somewhere in the middle. Based on our discussion, this is teaching us that there is still an element of Shabbat within the essential makeup of Pesach! Moreover, this combining of elements is particularly fitting for *Chumash Devarim* the way that we understand it,[22] for as the Torah "reviews" the contents of the first four *Chumashim*, it is fitting to refer to the *issur* of *melachah* on Pesach as it was presented both in *Chumash Shemot* ("*kol melachah*") as well as in *Chumash Vayikra* ("*melechet avodah*"). The way to combine both of these is with the one word — "*melachah*."

Further Connections

It is quite remarkable to see how this unique connection between Pesach and Shabbat expresses itself in other areas of Torah as well. Let us mention a few examples.

1. The Gemara in *Masechet Shabbat* (49b) quotes an opinion that the source in the Torah for the thirty-nine *avot melachah* on Shabbat is the fact that the word "*melachah*" appears thirty-nine times in the Torah. Rabbeinu Chananel there quotes the Yerushalmi that states that the thirty-ninth occurrence is in the *pasuk* regarding Pesach, which says "לֹא תֵעָשֶׂה כָל מְלָאכָה"! We see here that the *issur melachah* of Pesach is relevant as a contributing source to the *sugya* of *melachah* on Shabbat.

2. The Gemara in *Masechet Megillah* (13b) explains that when Haman said to Achashverosh (*Esther* 3:8), "וְאֶת דָּתֵי הַמֶּלֶךְ אֵינָם עֹשִׂים — and they do not fulfill the laws of the king," he was saying, "דְּמַפִּיק לְכוּלָא שַׁתָּא בשה"י פה"י — they spend the whole year saying 'shahi pahi,'" which Rashi explains as meaning that they would constantly say "*Shabbat hayom* (it is Shabbat today),

---

22   In the *sefer Kedushat Peshuto Shel Mikra*, this topic is discussed in *Parashat Devarim*.

Pesach hayom (it is Pesach today), and we are forbidden to do *melachah.*" We see here as well that the two days of Pesach and Shabbat are naturally referred to together.

3. The Gemara in *Masechet Pesachim* (85b), while discussing the *lo taaseh* of removing part of the *korban pesach* from the house,[23] states that one does not violate this *issur* until he places it down in its new location. The Gemara derives this through a *gezeirah shavah* from the *issur* of *hotza'ah* on Shabbat! The *Torah Temimah* (*Shemot* ibid.) has great difficulty in understanding how these two days are connected to the extent that we could learn *halachot* from one to the other. Based on our discussion, we can see that they are intimately connected!

And so, we have succeeded in learning from *peshuto shel mikra* that Pesach contains within it a "*Shabbosdik*" element that does not exist within the other *Mo'adim*, so that Pesach — and only Pesach — can be referred to as "Shabbat."[24]

---

23 See *Shemot* 12:46.
24 In the *sefer Kedushat Peshuto Shel Mikra*, the idea of "composite mitzvot" is discussed in *Parashat Tetzaveh* and *Parashat Tzav*. See also *Ma'amar Ten* in this *choveret*.

Ma'amar Three

PSHAT AND HALACHAH (i) –
HALACHAH L'SHA'AH

WE HAVE SEEN that whenever the *pshat* appears to give us an interpretation that differs from the halachah as we know it, we proceed to ask, "What *is* it that the *pshat* is teaching us, if it is not teaching us halachah?" The answer to that question will reveal a message that is part of the *shleimut* of Torah, even if it is not the halachah itself. In this *ma'amar* we will see that sometimes the *pshat* differs from the halachah, yet still it reflects halachah! How can this be? This brings us to the discussion of *halachah l'sha'ah* — halachah that was stated regarding a specific time.[25]

Avodat Yom HaKippurim —
The "Order" Written out of Order!

The first topic dealt with in *Parashat Acharei Mot* is the *Avodah* of the *Kohen Gadol* on Yom Kippur. And yet, as we will see, specifically in this *perek* — which is meant to tell us the *sequence* of the *Avodah* — Chazal inform us that there are *pesukim* that are written out of order!

---

25 In contrast to *halachah l'dorot* — halachah that applies to all future generations, which will be discussed in the following *ma'amar*.

וּבָא אַהֲרֹן אֶל אֹהֶל מוֹעֵד וּפָשַׁט אֶת בִּגְדֵי הַבָּד אֲשֶׁר לָבַשׁ בְּבֹאוֹ
אֶל הַקֹּדֶשׁ וְהִנִּיחָם שָׁם:

Aharon shall come to the Ohel Mo'ed (Mishkan), he shall
remove the linen garments that he wore when he entered the
Sanctuary, and he shall leave them there (Vayikra 16:23).

Chazal (*Yoma* 32a) ask why the *Kohen Gadol* is returning to the
Ohel Mo'ed at this point in the *Avodah* and explain that it is to remove the ladle and shovel with which he had brought *ketoret* into
the *Kodesh HaKodashim* earlier (as referred to in *pesukim* 12–13).
Regarding this, Chazal comment, "for the entire *parashah* is written
in order, except for this *pasuk*."

Before we try and clarify what we are meant to learn from this "incorrect" order of *pesukim*, since, after all, "*ain mikra yotzei midei peshuto*,"
and *peshuto shel mikra* requires us to read the *pesukim* in the order in
which they are written, we must first understand the basis upon which
Chazal determined that this *pasuk* describing the second visit of Aharon
to the *Kodesh HaKodashim* is written out of order. At the root of the
matter lies **kabbalat Chazal**, an oral tradition received by Chazal, which
states that during the *Avodah* on Yom Kippur, the *Kohen Gadol* immersed
himself in the *mikveh* five times and washed his hands and feet (*kiddush
yadayim v'raglayim*) ten times. The matter that requires each *tevilah* (and,
additionally, washing the hands and feet both before and after) is when
the *Kohen Gadol* changes into *bigdei zahav* (lit. golden garments — his
regular garments, which contain gold threads) or into *bigdei lavan* (lit.
white garments — the special garments for Yom Kippur made entirely
of white linen). Were the order of the *Avodah* to follow the order of the
pesukim, there would only be three such changes (gold, white, and gold),
and hence only three immersions in the *mikveh* and six washings of the
hands and feet. In order to arrive at a total of five changes of garments,
we must "detach" *pasuk* 23 from where it was written and place it at the
end of the *parashah*, after *pasuk* 28. In this way there will be two more
changes of clothing (from white to gold and from gold to white), which

will then give us two more immersions and four more washings of the hands and feet.

Rashi's Words of Clarification

Rashi, in his comments on our *pesukim*, explains the matter in his characteristic clear manner (*pasuk* 23, s.v. *u'pashat*):

> *The entire parashah is written in order except for this [second] entrance [to the Kodesh HaKodashim], which actually took place after Aharon brought his olah and the olah of the people, and offered the sacrificial parts of the bull and goat, all of those things being done while wearing the bigdei zahav. Then he immerses in the mikveh, washes his hands and feet, removes those garments, and wears the bigdei lavan in order to remove the ladle and shovel with which he had offered ketoret in the Kodesh HaKodashim. He then removes the bigdei lavan and wears bigdei zahav for the afternoon korban tamid. Here is the Seder Ha'Avodah:*
>
> - *The morning tamid — wearing **gold**.*
> - *The avodot of the bull and goat inside the Kodesh HaKodashim, as well as offering the ketoret there — wearing **white**.*
> - *Offering the Kohen's ram and the ram of the people, plus offering some of the mussafim — wearing **gold**.*
> - *Removing the ladle and the shovel from the Kodesh HaKodashim — wearing **white**.*
> - *Offering the rest of the mussafim and the afternoon tamid, plus the ketoret of the Heichal on the Inner Mizbey'ach — wearing **gold**.*
>
> *In terms of the order of the Avodah, the order of the pesukim would be as follows:*
>
> - *Sending away the goat to the wilderness (pasuk 22).*
> - *Immersing in the mikveh (pasuk 24).*

- *Offering his olah, the olah of the people, and all the items mentioned in the subsequent four pesukim (pesukim 24–28).*
- **And then** *returning to remove the ladle and the shovel (pasuk 23).*

The Vilna Gaon — the *Seder Ha'Avodah* According to *Pshat*

Now let us return to our question. If in fact the *Kohen Gadol* actually requires five *tevilot*, why does the Torah write it as if he only needs three, which then requires us to move a *pasuk* from its "incorrect" place, when we do not understand what it was doing there in the first place! Or, to put it in the words of the *Chochmat Adam*, "Is the Torah not able to order the *pesukim* as Rashi did?" This is in essence a very extreme way of phrasing the question, "*madua* — why?" As we have explained on a number of occasions, the question of "*madua*" follows the question of "*keytzad* — how?" When the midrash of Chazal differs from *peshuto shel mikra*, we first ask [Chazal], "*Keytzad* — How did you know to expound the *pasuk* in the way that you did?" and then we ask [Hashem, so to speak], "*Madua* — Why did You dictate to Moshe a *pasuk* whose *pshat* differs from the way in which You explained the halachah to him?"

The **Chochmat Adam**, the *gaon* R' Avraham Danzig,[26] gives the following answer:

> It appears to me, based on what I heard from **Moreinu Ve'Rabbeinu the Gaon and Chassid R' Eliyahu of Vilna**... based on a statement of the Midrash Rabbah in our parashah (21:7), "Said Rav Yudan bar Simon, Moshe suffered great distress when he was told regarding Aharon "וְאַל יָבֹא בְכָל עֵת אֶל הַקֹּדֶשׁ" — he shall not enter the Kodesh [HaKodashim] at all times" (pasuk 2). A "time" (עֵת) might mean an hour, a day, a year, twelve years, seventy years,

---

26   [Author of *Chayei Adam*.]

forever! Said Hashem to Moshe, 'It is not as you think...
rather, whenever he wants he may enter, provided he en-
ters with the following order (of korbanot).'"

We see from here that it is specifically later Kohanim Gedolim
who are restricted from entering the Kodesh HaKodashim
aside from on Yom Kippur. Aharon, however, was able to
enter at any time, provided he did so accompanied by the
korbanot mentioned in the parashah. According to this, we
*see that **the Torah was most precise with the order of the***
***pesukim,** for the reason the Gemara said that pasuk 23 is*
*written "out of order" is as a result of the **kabbalah** that the*
Kohen Gadol needs five tevilot on Yom Kippur, whereas in
the pesukim as they are written we find only three. However,
*this is only in regard to **Yom Kippur,** when we have this*
tradition handed down to Moshe at Sinai that he needs five
tevilot. However, with regards to Aharon being able to enter
*on **other days of the year,** there is no such requirement. This*
being the case, he only needed to immerse three times, as
per the order that the pesukim are written in the parashah.
And if this is the case, then the pasuk of "Aharon shall enter"
(pasuk 23) is written in order, in regard to Aharon on any
other day of the year!

Resolving Questions in *Peshuto Shel Mikra*

Having quoted the interpretation of the Vilna Gaon, the **Chochmat**
Adam then shows how this approach will not only explain how the
pesukim may be read in order, but will also resolve some very basic
questions that relate to *peshuto shel mikra* in our *perek*:

1. Based on the above distinction between Aharon and subse-
    quent *Kohanim Gedolim*, we can understand why there is no
    mention at all of Yom Kippur at the beginning of the *parashah*;
    rather, it is only mentioned at the end! Every *parashah* of the

korbanot for a *Mo'ed* begins first by mentioning the date of the *Mo'ed* and then saying which *korbanot* are to be brought on that day. Why is *Avodat Yom Kippur* different? The answer is, since *lefi peshuto* this *parashah* reflects the *seder* of Aharon on any day of the year, Yom Kippur is not mentioned. It is only at the end of the *parashah* that the Torah states that this *Seder Ha'Avodah* is required for all subsequent generations on Yom Kippur.

2. We can further understand why it is that throughout this *perek* the Torah refers to "Aharon," whereas in the final *pesukim* it no longer mentions his name, but rather "the Kohen who shall be anointed [*Kohen Gadol*]." This is because these final *pesukim* are no longer dealing with the *Avodah* in the *Mishkan* that could be done by Aharon on any day, but rather with *Yom HaKippurim l'dorot*, which is done by the *Kohen Gadol*.

3. The final words of the *perek* (*pasuk* 34) read, "וַיַּעַשׂ כַּאֲשֶׁר צִוָּה ה' אֶת מֹשֶׁה — and [Aharon] did as Hashem commanded Moshe." These words seem superfluous, for is it not obvious that Aharon would do as Hashem commanded Moshe?[27] According to the Vilna Gaon, these words can be understood *lefi peshuto* — namely, that although Yom Kippur was yet months away, Aharon **immediately** began to enter the *Kodesh HaKodashim*, as he was entitled to, provided he followed the *Seder Ha'Avodah* as mentioned in the *parashah*.

We thus have before us two distinct categories regarding entering the *Kodesh HaKodashim*.

1. Aharon, who may enter at any time during the course of the year, provided he brings the *korbanot* mentioned in the *parashah*.

2. The *Kohen Gadol* on Yom Kippur *l'dorot* (including Aharon on Yom Kippur in the *Midbar*), accompanied by the special *Seder Ha'Avodah* received by Chazal (five *tevilot*).[28]

---

27 [See Rashi's comment there.]

28 In fact there is a third category, as discussed in the *Torat Kohanim* (*Parashat Acharei Mot*),

The approach of the Vilna Gaon is also found in the *peirush Haamek Davar* of the Netziv, as if it is practically self-understood from the *pesukim* themselves (*pasuk* 23, s.v. *u'va*):

> According to the pshat, the pasuk is referring specifically to Aharon, that is, if he wants to enter the Ohel Mo'ed, it must be after all these preparations. However, all this is only true regarding Aharon, but for subsequent generations, the pasuk must be understood as referring to "removing the ladle and the shovel," as the Gemara explains.

Why Was the Halachah Different in Aharon's Time?

We have seen regarding the opening section of *Acharei Mot* that *halachah l'sha'ah* is expressed by *peshuto shel mikra*, whereas *halachah l'dorot* is derived through *Torah SheBaal Peh*. However, we still need to explain why, when it comes to the *Avodah* of Yom Kippur, would Aharon's status in the *Midbar* be any different than that of the *Kohen Gadol l'dorot*?

In answering this question, the **Meshech Chochmah** refers to us a comment of the *Seforno* at the end of *Parashat Emor* (*Vayikra* 24:3, s.v. *ya'aroch oto Aharon*). There, the *Seforno* addresses the fact that although the lighting of the Menorah does not need to be done by a *Kohen Gadol* specifically, nonetheless, the *pasuk* makes specific reference to Aharon when it describes the lighting:

> Even though kindling the lights of the Menorah can be done by a regular Kohen (hedyot) in subsequent generations, nonetheless, the pasuk refers to Aharon. For indeed, **the entire time that Bnei Yisrael were in the Midbar, the level of the Mishkan was that which would be achieved in**

---

namely, Moshe, who is able to enter the *Kodesh HaKodashim* whenever he wants without any *Seder Ha'Avodah*, for "Aharon may not enter at any time [without *korbanot*], but Moshe may enter at any time" (*Torat Kohanim* ibid.).

*subsequent generations [only] on Yom Kippur. Therefore,
it was fitting that the kindling of the lights be done by the
Kohen Gadol, as is the case l'dorot on Yom Kippur.*

Based on the *Seforno*, the *Meshech Chochmah* explains how it was
possible for Aharon to enter the *Kodesh HaKodashim* at any time, not
just on Yom Kippur, for during the time of the *Midbar*, the Mishkan
was on the *madreigah* of Yom Kippur on an ongoing basis!

The *Meshech Chochmah* then goes further and explains not only
how it was **possible** for Aharon to enter at any time, but also why it
was **necessary.** After all, if the Torah indicates that Aharon *could* enter
at any time, it seems as if there was in fact a need for him to do so:

*As long as Yisrael were in the Midbar, it was forbidden for
them to eat basar taavah (ordinary meat that was not a
korban), which means that they were constantly eating meat
that was kodesh. This meant that tumah of the Mikdash and
kodesh items was much more prevalent, and thus required
kaparah more frequently. This is why Aharon would enter "בְּכָל
עֵת — at any time" with the Avodah prescribed for the day, in
order to atone for tumah of the Mikdash and kodesh items.*

We should note that although the *Meshech Chochmah* has provided
a potential source for the approach of the Vilna Gaon, the two might
not be exactly the same. The Vilna Gaon seems to be saying that the
possibility of Aharon entering the *Kodesh HaKodashim* is a function
of the unique status of **Aharon.** The *Meshech Chochmah*, on the other hand, explained that it is a function of the unique status of **the
Mishkan** in the *Midbar*. In case we think that these are two ways of
saying the same thing, we should remind ourselves that for the final
eight months of our time in the *Midbar*, it was Aharon's son, Elazar,
who was *Kohen Gadol*. What was Elazar's status? Was he also able to
enter at any time? Here it would appear that the two approaches part
ways. If it was Aharon who was unique, as the words of the Gaon seem

to indicate, then Elazar would be like any subsequent *Kohen Gadol*, and could only enter on Yom Kippur. However, according to the *Meshech Chochmah*, the determining factor is the *madreigah* of the Mishkan in the *Midbar*, and this *madreigah* continued to exist during those final eight months, when Elazar was *Kohen Gadol*.

A Source in the Gemara for *Halachah L'Sha'ah*

Following the approach of the Vilna Gaon, **R' Yaakov Kamenetzky** writes in his *peirush* **Emet L'Yaakov** (*Vayikra* 16:2, s.v. *v'al*):

> It is possible that he [the Gaon] derived this from the fact that the Gemara (Gittin 60a) states that eight parshiyot were given over on the day the Mishkan was erected and lists one of them as the parashah of Avodat Yom HaKippurim. Rashi there senses a difficulty with this and comments, "Even though this parashah applies to Yom Kippur,[29] nonetheless it was said on that day." However, according to the explanation of the Vilna Gaon, it is well understood, for in reality the parashah did not apply only to Yom Kippur; rather, whenever Aharon wished to enter the Kodesh HaKodashim he would need to perform the Seder Ha'Avodah that was required on Yom Kippur, therefore it was said on that (first) day.

In the Future

Let us take this discussion one stage further and ask a most interesting question: Is it possible that the ability to enter the *Kodesh HaKodashim* on a day other than Yom Kippur will ever return?

R' Meir Don Plotzki, the author of **Kli Chemdah** on the Torah, writes (beginning of *Parashat Acharei Mot*):

> It seems to me that even though this special level existed only in connection with Aharon, whereas any other Kohen

---

29   [Whereas the Mishkan was set up on the first day of Nissan, six months *before* Yom Kippur.]

Gadol was not allowed to enter the Kodesh HaKodashim except on Yom Kippur, nonetheless, since we see that Aharon was able to enter whenever he wanted if accompanied by this Avodah, and similarly **in the future** *[at the time of Techiyat HaMeitim] when Moshe and Aharon will return, Aharon will [once again] be allowed to enter accompanied by this Seder Ha'Avodah. It is with regards to other Kohanim, whose level is not as great, that the Torah writes that they "may not enter at any time" except for on Yom Kippur. If so, it appears that these korbanot are not to be classified as "chovat hayom" —* **obligations of the day of Yom Kippur per se***; rather, they are the korbanot that are a necessary accompaniment for anyone who is eligible to enter the Kodesh HaKodashim.*

In other words, *peshuto shel mikra* ("With this **Aharon** shall enter **the Kodesh**") teaches us that this special *Seder Ha'Avodah* (*korbanot, tevilot*, washing of the hands and feet) is in essence a requirement of entering the *Kodesh HaKodashim* and not a requirement of Yom Kippur; it is just that it is an *Avodah* that must be performed once a year — on Yom Kippur. If so, then instead of referring to the "*Seder Ha'Avodah* of Yom Kippur," it may be more correct to refer to the "*Seder Ha'Avodah* of entering the *Kodesh HaKodashim*."

During the time Bnei Yisrael were in the *Midbar*, the level of *kedushah* was so great throughout the course of the year that a *Kohen Gadol* who was on the level of Aharon (and perhaps Elazar)[30] could enter the *Kodesh HaKodashim* whenever he wanted, accompanied by the *Seder Ha'Avodah* as set forth according to *peshuto shel mikra*. From that point onward (after Bnei Yisrael entered the Land), in the absence of that special level of *kedushah* on the one hand, and the

---

30   [The *Kli Chemdah* quoted above made specific reference to Aharon; however, the Rav is leaving open the possibility that the determining factor was the time in the *Midbar*, which would then also include Elazar.]

absence of a *Kohen Gadol* as holy as Aharon on the other hand, entering the *Kodesh HaKodashim* became restricted to once a year, on the unique day of Yom Kippur, while the *Seder Ha'Avodah* changed to five *tevilot* instead of three.

Nevertheless, the *Kli Chemdah* states that in the future it will once again be possible for Aharon to enter at any time. Moreover, according to the approach of the *Meshech Chochmah* based on the *Seforno*, we see that the level of *kedushah* in the Mishkan on a normal weekday was equal to the *kedushah* that existed in the *Beit HaMikdash* on Yom Kippur. If so, then this level will certainly exist in the third *Beit HaMikdash*, whose level of *kedushah,* the *Seforno* (*Parashat Pekudei*) tells us, will be greatest of all, and the *Kohen Gadol* will enjoy the same status of Aharon HaKohen, with all that that implies.

Thus we have before us a unique situation where *peshuto shel mikra* reflects the halachah as it applied *l'sha'ah* (in the *Midbar*), but not *l'dorot* (after entering the Land); nonetheless, it may also reflect a possible expression of *halachah lemaaseh* in the future, with the rebuilding of the *Beit HaMikdash*.

Ma'amar Four

PSHAT AND HALACHAH (2) –
HALACHAH L'DOROT

SO FAR WE have seen that even when *peshuto shel mikra* differs
from the halachah as we know it from the midrash, it can nonetheless reflect the halachah in terms of the way it was at that time
period — *halachah l'sha'ah*, while the midrash reflects the *halachah
l'dorot*. However, as we shall now see, it is also possible for the *pshat*
to differ from the halachah as derived by the midrash and yet still
reflect *halachah l'dorot*.

"Lo Yumtu Avot Al Banim" in Pshat and in Drash

The *pasuk* in *Sefer Devarim* (24:16) states:

לֹא יוּמְתוּ אָבוֹת עַל בָּנִים וּבָנִים לֹא יוּמְתוּ עַל אָבוֹת אִישׁ
בְּחֶטְאוֹ יוּמָתוּ:

The straightforward meaning of these words in terms of *peshuto
shel mikra* would seem to be that fathers shall not be killed **on account** of the sins of their sons and vice versa. However, the *midrash
halachah* (*Sanhedrin* 27b) explains the *pasuk* as saying that sons
should not be put to death on the basis of **the testimony** of their

50

fathers! In other words, this *pasuk* is looked upon as the source for the disqualification of close family members testifying about each other. Nevertheless, in *Sefer Melachim* (II, 14:6), when describing how Amatziah HaMelech killed those responsible for murdering his father, the *pasuk* states:

וְאֶת בְּנֵי הַמַּכִּים לֹא הֵמִית כַּכָּתוּב בְּסֵפֶר תּוֹרַת מֹשֶׁה אֲשֶׁר צִוָּה
ה' לֵאמֹר לֹא יוּמְתוּ אָבוֹת עַל בָּנִים וּבָנִים לֹא יוּמְתוּ עַל אָבוֹת כִּי
אִם אִישׁ בְּחֶטְאוֹ יוּמָת:

*He did not kill the sons of those who killed [his father], as
it is written in the book of Torat Moshe, which Hashem
commanded, saying, "Fathers shall not be killed because
of their sons, and sons shall not be killed because of their
fathers, rather, a person shall be killed for his own sin."*

This *pasuk* reveals something quite remarkable. Many, many, generations after *Matan Torah*, a halachah is presented as being based on *peshuto shel mikra*, while the *midrash halachah* explains those same words in a completely different manner!

Commenting on this phenomenon, the **Ran** writes (***Chiddushei HaRan***, *Sanhedrin* ibid):

*If you ask, how can the Gemara explain that the pasuk refers
to testimony of family members, is it not rather needed for
its literal meaning, that sons shouldn't die on account of
their fathers, as we find with regards to Amatziah where
it says, "He did not kill the sons of those who killed etc."?
The answer is, the pasuk does not depart from its literal
meaning, and the **pshat** of the pasuk is that sons should
not die **on account** of their fathers, and its **midrash** is that
they should not die based on **the testimony** of their fathers;
and one pasuk can yield numerous meanings as it states
(Tehillim 62:12), "אַחַת דִּבֶּר אֱלֹקִים שְׁתַּיִם זוּ שָׁמָעְתִּי" — Hashem
has proclaimed one thing, and I have heard two."*

Establishing Parameters for Deriving Halachah from *Pshat*

At this point we may ask, how does this fit in with what we have learned until now? We have seen, based on numerous examples, that whenever the *pshat* and the *drash* differ, the halachah is as the midrash states, and the *pshat* is taken as teaching us a Torah message that is not halachic. Yet here we see that we are learning *halachah l'dorot* from *pshat*, even when it differs from the *drash*!

R' Yaakov Tzvi Mecklenberg, in his *peirush HaKetav VeHakabbalah* (*Devarim* ibid.), provides us with a basic guideline. In the previous cases that we have seen, the *pshat* and the midrash **contradict** each other. If the punishment for putting out someone's eye is paying him for it, then it is not putting out the aggressor's eye, for he is certainly not to be punished twice! If the *Omer* is to be counted from the second day of Pesach, then it is not to be counted from Sunday! If the *Kohen Gadol* needs to immerse in the *mikveh* five times on Yom Kippur, then three times are not enough! In these cases where the *pshat* is in conflict with the midrash, we take the halachah from the midrash and look to the *pshat* for a different type of Torah lesson or, alternatively, understand it as reflecting *halachah l'sha'ah*. Regarding our *pasuk* of "*lo yumtu*," however, there is **no contradiction whatsoever** between the halachah as derived by midrash and that which is communicated through *pshat*. Saying that a son should not die on account of the sins of his father doesn't mean that he should be killed based on his testimony; they are simply two different *halachot* in two completely different realms, and, if we may say, never the twain shall meet! In this case, there is no reason to abandon the *pshat* as a source of halachah, even as the midrash derives a different halachah from the very same words. Additionally, in this case the **Gemara itself** did not consider the meaning of the *pasuk al pi peshuto* ("on account of fathers") to be halachically unacceptable, it simply pointed out that this halachah is written explicitly in the final phrase of the *pasuk*, "אִישׁ בְּחֶטְאוֹ יוּמָתוּ — a person shall be killed for his own sin," and it is unlikely that the *pasuk* is merely saying the same thing twice! However, this does not negate the simple meaning based on *peshuto shel mikra* in the first part of the *pasuk*, and, in this case, it continues to teach *halachah l'dorot*.

Matzah during Pesach

Taking the discussion one stage further, as we will see, not only do we find *peshuto shel mikra* teaching us *halachah d'Oraita l'dorot* in an area that is distinct from the *midrash halachah* [for example, sins of the fathers vs. testimony of the fathers], the *pshat* can even teach us *halachah l'dorot* regarding the very topic being discussed by the *midrash halachah* and yet still teach us a different aspect of the halachah.

Regarding eating matzah on Pesach, the Torah writes (*Shemot* 12:15), "שִׁבְעַת יָמִים מַצּוֹת תֹּאכֵלוּ" — for seven days you shall eat *matzot*." Nonetheless, the *midrash halachah* tells us that there is only a *chiyuv* to eat matzah on the first night of Pesach.[31] For the rest of the seven days, eating matzah is classified as "*reshut*" which literally means "optional." The basis of this halachah is one of R' Yishmael's Thirteen Principles for deriving halachah, which teaches that when something is initially part of a *klal* (general rule), and then is mentioned by itself apart from the *klal* in order to teach a new halachah, this serves not only to teach that halachah regarding the specifically mentioned item alone, but rather to teach it regarding the entire *klal*. Thus, although the *pasuk* in *Shemot* says to eat matzah for **seven** days, a different *pasuk* (*Devarim* 16:8) says to eat matzah for **six** days, which renders the seventh day as being excluded from the mitzvah. This then teaches us that in fact **all seven days** are excluded from the obligation of eating matzah! The special mitzvah of eating matzah on the first night of Pesach is derived from a separate *pasuk* (*Shemot* 12: 18) that says "בָּעֶרֶב תֹּאכְלוּ מַצֹּת" — on the evening [of the first night of Pesach] you shall eat *matzot*."

This entire situation leaves us with a basic question — namely, if indeed there is no mitzvah to eat matzah apart from the first night of Pesach, why, then, did the Torah write that we should eat matzah for seven days, which then required it to "unwrite" it so that there

---

31   See Rashi *Shemot* ibid., quoting the *Mechilta*.

is no mitzvah at all? Or, to put it differently, the halachic arithmetic regarding this mitzvah seems to state that 7 + 6 = 0![32]

From the words of the **Vilna Gaon**[33] we may deduce an answer to this question on the level of *pshat*:

> During the entire seven days of Pesach, eating matzah is a mitzvah; the Gemara only calls it "reshut" in contrast to the first night, which is a chovah (obligation). A "mitzvah" relative to a "chovah" is called "reshut." Nevertheless, it is a mitzvah d'Oraita.[34]

Here we see that *midrash halachah* and *peshuto shel mikra* are telling us different things about the very same mitzvah, and both of them are *halachah d'Oraita*! The *midrash halachah* determines that there is no *chiyuv* to eat matzah after the first night of Pesach. At the same time, the fact remains that the *pasuk* stated explicitly that we are to eat matzah for all seven days, which on the level of *pshat* clearly sounds like a mitzvah! The Vilna Gaon explains that the *midrash halachah* relates to the *chiyuv* of matzah, whereas *peshuto shel mikra* teaches us that even if there is no *chiyuv* during the seven days, there is nonetheless a mitzvah, and it is a *mitzvah d'Oraita*.

Eved Ivri

In discussing the case of an *eved ivri* who chooses to stay on beyond the basic term of six years, the Torah states (*Shemot* 21:6):

$$\text{וְרָצַע אֲדֹנָיו אֶת אָזְנוֹ בַּמַּרְצֵעַ וַעֲבָדוֹ לְעֹלָם}$$

His master shall pierce his ear with an awl, and he shall serve him forever.

---

32 See *Pesachim* 38b and *Menachot* 66a where the Gemara raises this question and explains how further *halachot* are derived from the Torah having written the mitzvah in this way.

33 *Maaseh Rav*, *siman* 185.

34 [This relates to a category of *mitzvot* known as "מצוה קיומית," where there is no obligation to perform this act. However, one who does so fulfills a mitzvah. This is in contrast to "מצוה חיובית" (the category to which most *mitzvot* apply) where there is an actual obligation.]

Two Approaches in the *Rishonim* to *"L'Olam"* — until the *Yovel*

Commenting on the words "עֲבָדוֹ לְעֹלָם — *and he shall serve him forever*," **Rashi** says:

עַד הַיּוֹבֵל. אוֹ אֵינוֹ אֶלָּא לְעוֹלָם כְּמַשְׁמָעוֹ? תַּלְמוּד לוֹמַר (ויקרא כה,י): "וְאִישׁ אֶל מִשְׁפַּחְתּוֹ תָּשֻׁבוּ", מַגִּיד שֶׁחֲמִשִּׁים שָׁנָה קְרוּיִם "עוֹלָם."

Until the Yovel.[35] Or perhaps [it means literally] "forever" as the word implies?[36] To this end the pasuk states elsewhere[37] (Vayikra 25:10), "and each man shall return to his family." This teaches us that fifty years is called "l'olam."[38]

We see that Rashi's way of arriving at the conclusion that *"l'olam"* means "until the *Yovel*" comes from taking into account a parallel *pasuk* in *Vayikra* that states that all men, i.e., including the *eved ivri*, return home in the *Yovel*. A different approach toward arriving at this conclusion is found in **Rabbeinu Bachye**[39] (s.v. *va'avado*):

Chazal received a tradition that the word "l'olam" here refers to the "olam" of Yovel, i.e., fifty years, for the time span of fifty years is called "l'olam."[40] For thus we find regarding Shmuel HaRamati[41] (Shmuel I, 1:22), "וְיָשַׁב שָׁם עַד עוֹלָם — he shall stay there forever," referring to the "olam" of a Levi,

---

35   It is Rashi's way to first state the correct interpretation and then proceed to raise other alternatives and demonstrate why they are not appropriate.

36   Rashi does not refer to this *peirush* as *"k'peshuto,"* since no one lives forever; rather, he calls it *"k'mashma'o,"* namely, for the rest of his life.

37   Regarding the *Yovel* year.

38   Note that Rashi does not conclude that the lesson is one of halachah, i.e., that the *eved* goes free at the *Yovel*, but rather it is one of *Lashon HaKodesh*, that the word *"olam"* can also mean fifty years.

39   Based on the words of the Ramban, the *rebbe* of the Rashba, who in turn was the *rebbe* of Rabbeinu Bachye.

40   I.e., even not within the context of *eved ivri*.

41   [Said by his mother, Chanah.]

who serves in the Mikdash until the age of fifty.[42] *The days
of Shmuel numbered fifty-two years (Yerushalmi Berachot
4:1), and he was two years old at that time.*[43] *Since a Levi
serves until the "Yovel" year,*[44] *it transpires that he [Shmuel]
served all the days of that "olam."*

According to Rabbeinu Bachye, the definition of "*l'olam*" as fifty
years can be traced back to *pesukim* in *Nevi'im* that were not stated
within the context of *eved ivri* or the *Yovel* year, but rather were
describing the *avodah* of *Levi'im* and the lifespan of Shmuel. [It is
worthwhile to point out in this regard that nowhere in the *pasuk* do
we find a reference to the fact that Shmuel lived for fifty-two years,
so that this *limud* is based on *pesukim* but still relies on a *kabbalah*.]

Learning Halachah from *"L'Olam" Al Pi Peshuto*

At the same time as Chazal have explained *al pi midrasho* that the
word "*l'olam*" means "until the *Yovel*," we find that it can also teach us
halachah when understood *lefi peshuto* as meaning "permanently."
Thus, for example, we find in the **Mechilta of R' Shimon ben Yochai:**[45]

"וְשַׁבְתֶּם אִישׁ אֶל אֲחֻזָּתוֹ וְאִישׁ אֶל מִשְׁפַּחְתּוֹ תָּשֻׁבוּ" —
זֶה הַנִּרְצָע לִפְנֵי הַיּוֹבֵל שֶׁהַיּוֹבֵל מוֹצִיאוֹ, וּמַה תַּלְמוּד לוֹמַר
"וַעֲבָדוֹ לְעוֹלָם" — כָּל יְמֵי עוֹלָמוֹ שֶׁל רוֹצֵעַ.

*"You shall return each man to his inheritance, and each
man shall return to his family" — this refers to one whose
ear was pierced before the Yovel, that the Yovel year sets
him free. What, then, is the meaning of [the pasuk] "va'avado l'olam"? This refers to the "olam" (lifetime) of* **the one
who pierced his ear.**

---

42   *Bamidbar* 8:24.

43   I.e., that his mother said that he should stay "*ad olam*."

44   I.e., until his fiftieth year.

45   [This is a different work of *midrash halachah* on *Chumash Shemot* than the one commonly
referred to as "the *Mechilta*," which was authored by R' Yishmael.]

Until this point we saw the two terms of *"l'olam"* and *"ad haYovel"* as both referring to the *eved ivri*, which then led us, through *midrash halachah*, to explain *"l'olam"* as meaning until the *Yovel*. According to the *Mechilta* of R' Shimon ben Yochai, we learn a separate halachah from the word *"l'olam" k'peshuto*, namely, that the *eved ivri* goes free if the master dies, for the word *"l'olam"* is taken as referring to the *"olam,"* that is, lifespan, of the master![46]

The *Meshech Chochmah's* Approach

Another way of seeing the word *"l'olam"* as teaching us halachah on the level of *pshat* is discussed by the *Sar HaTorah*, R' Meir Simcha HaKohen (based on the Ramban), who explains that *"l'olam"* can mean "for the rest of his life" even if it refers to **the eved**! How can this be? Do we not have a *kabbalah* from Chazal that the *eved* goes free in the *Yovel* year? The *Meshech Chochmah* explains (s.v. *va'avado*):

> It is worthwhile investigating the status of an eved ivri who was sold at a time when the Yovel applied, and within the first six years of his term the Yovel was discontinued — as was the case when the Ten Shevatim went into exile — so that there were no longer "כָּל יוֹשְׁבֶיהָ עָלֶיהָ — all of its inhabitants upon it."[47] Since the law of eved ivri only applies when the Yovel is in force, do we say that in this case his servitude expires?[48] Or do we say that he remains an eved, as is the case with an "ancestral field"?[49] If so, the only thing that

---

46   The implications for reading the phrase "וַעֲבָדוֹ לְעוֹלָם — *and* **he** *[the eved] shall serve* **him** *[the master] forever [for the rest of his life]*," is that the "life" being referred to ("his life") is not that of the *eved* — the subject, but of the master — the object.

47   I.e., living in the land of Israel, which is a requirement for the *Yovel* year to be in effect. See Rambam *Hilchot Shemittah V'Yovel* 10:8.

48   [I.e., immediately, even before six years are up.]

49   Such a field would normally return to its original owner in the *Yovel* year (see *Vayikra* 25:25–28). However, in the event that the *Yovel* was discontinued, the field would become the permanent property of the purchaser.

could set him free[50] *would be the Yovel — if it applied, for
with that the Torah releases him. However, if there was no
longer a Yovel, then he would remain an eved "l'olam" — as
long as the master lives.*[51] *Therefore, the words "וַעֲבָדוֹ לְעוֹלָם"
are entirely accurate lefi peshuto, for he does indeed need to
serve the master forever, it is just that if there is a Yovel, it
will release him — understand this well. See Tosafot Arachin
33a, s.v. ela*[52] *and Ramban Gittin 36a*[53] *regarding pruzbul.*

We see here a situation where *peshuto shel mikra* ["l'olam" as per-
manent] teaches a *halachah d'Oraita* parallel to — and not in conflict
with — the halachah as derived by *midrash halachah* [Yovel releases
the *eved*], so that *eilu v'eilu* — both of them are words of *halachah
d'Oraita*, with each one operating under different circumstances.

---

50   [I.e., after six years.]

51   Here, the *Meshech Chochmah* has independently arrived at the same conclusion expressed by
the *Mechilta* of R' Shimon ben Yochai (mentioned above), which was not available in print in
his time.

52   Tosafot also seem to understand that the *Yovel* is in some way undoing the permanent term
implied by the word *"l'olam."*

53   S.v. *ha d'tanya*; "It further seems that if one acquired an *eved* during the time of the *Bayit*
(that is, *Beit HaMikdash*, during the times that the *Yovel* applies) and his ear was pierced
(i.e., he stayed past the first six years), and then the *Bayit* was destroyed and the *Yovel* was
discontinued before he was released, that he would remain an *eved 'l'olam* — permanently,'
and would retain the status of *eved ivri* who is allowed to marry a *shifchah Cana'anit.*"

SIGNON HAKATUV

Section B

INTRODUCTION

A BASIC AXIOM for anyone who learns Torah *al taharat ha-kodesh* is that there is no happenstance ("*mikriyut*") when it comes to the way the Torah is written. Based on this axiom, when we detect different ways in which the Torah presents things, we are entitled — and perhaps even required — to ask whether there are any differences between the various types of *signon* — styles or modes of expression. For example, is there a difference between something the Torah *commands*, as opposed to something that it *describes*? In a similar vein, we may ask, is there a difference between something the Torah itself says, as opposed to something it quotes someone else as saying?

We know that in terms of *kedushat haTorah* there is no question that every word is of equal value, and a *Sefer Torah* that is missing even one letter from any section is completely *pasul*, regardless of *signon*. Nonetheless, we still ask, is there any difference — within the *kedushah* and *shleimut* of Torah — between these different types of *signon*, whether in terms of their parameters or the way we are meant to understand what they are trying to teach us? This question will be the subject of the next two *ma'amarim*.

Ma'amar Five

LASHON TZIVUI VS. LASHON SIPPUR – IMPERATIVE FORM VS. NARRATIVE FORM

Part I: In Halachah —
the Source for the Mitzvah of Tefillah

ANYONE WHO IS asked the question, "What is the source for the mitzvah of *tefillah* in the Torah?" will probably respond by quoting three words from *Parashat Eikev* (11:13), "וּלְעָבְדוֹ בְּכָל לְבַבְכֶם — *and to serve Him with all your heart*," adding the comment of the *Sifrei*, "this refers to *tefillah*." To support this teaching we would cite the words of the Gemara in *Masechet Taanit* (2a), "אֵיזוֹ הִיא עֲבוֹדָה שֶׁבַּלֵּב? זוֹ תְּפִלָּה — *what is 'avodah of the heart'? This is tefillah*." However, when we consult the words of the **Rambam,** we will see that while the above sources may give us the **definition** of the mitzvah, they do not constitute a Torah **commandment** to fulfill the mitzvah. The Rambam (*Hilchot Tefillah* 1:1) says:

It is a positive mitzvah from the Torah to pray every day,[54]

---

54   This is as opposed to the opinion of the Ramban, who does not count the mitzvah of *tefillah* in the list of the *Taryag*.

as it says (Shemot 23:25), "וַעֲבַדְתֶּם אֵת ה' אֱלֹהֵיכֶם — *you shall serve Hashem, your God.*" *Through tradition we have learned that the "avodah" here refers to tefillah, as it says,* "וּלְעָבְדוֹ בְּכָל לְבַבְכֶם," *and the Chachamim explained (Taanit 2a) that this refers to tefillah.*

R' Yosef Karo, in his *peirush* **Kesef Mishneh**, asks a question:

> *Why did the Rambam not write that the source of the mitzvah is from the words* "וּלְעָבְדוֹ בְּכָל לְבַבְכֶם," *which explicitly refers to the mitzvah of tefillah?*

In other words, the question is, why did the Rambam mention the *pasuk* of "וַעֲבַדְתֶּם," which does not refer explicitly to *tefillah*, and then bring another *pasuk* that clarifies that the *avodah* here is in the heart, i.e., *tefillah*, when he could have simply just brought the *pasuk* of "וּלְעָבְדוֹ בְּכָל לְבַבְכֶם" itself, which would have told us everything?

The *Kesef Mishneh* answers:

> *The reason is because the pasuk of* "וּלְעָבְדוֹ" *is not a mitzvah — a* **commandment***, but rather sippur devarim — a* **narration***;* — וְהָיָה אִם שָׁמֹעַ תִּשְׁמְעוּ... לְאַהֲבָה אֵת ה' אֱלֹהֵיכֶם וּלְעָבְדוֹ... וְנָתַתִּי מְטַר אַרְצְכֶם *If you will listen... to love Hashem your God and to serve Him... and I will provide rain for your land.*

The fundamental principle we are being taught here is that a mitzvah of the Torah can only be derived from a *pasuk* that is phrased as **a commandment**.

This is something that Rambam has set forth in the eighth of the fourteen *shorashim* with which he prefaced his *Sefer HaMitzvot*:

> *It is not possible to introduce a commandment [that is to say, a positive mitzvah] within a pasuk of narrative... and similarly, a prohibition will not appear within a narrative.*

The *Sefer HaChinuch*

In a similar vein, the *Sefer HaChinuch* (Mitzvah 3) takes great care in explaining to us how to read the *pasuk* regarding the prohibition of *gid hanasheh* (Bereishit 32:33), "...עַל כֵּן לֹא יֹאכְלוּ בְנֵי יִשְׂרָאֵל אֶת גִּיד הַנָּשֶׁה. עַד הַיּוֹם הַזֶּה — *therefore, Bnei Yisrael will not eat the gid hanasheh... until this day*." These are his words:

> Not to eat from the gid hanasheh, as it says "therefore, Bnei Yisrael will not eat the gid hanasheh." These words "לֹא יֹאכְלוּ — *they will not eat*" were not said as a narrative, as if to say that since this episode happened to the father, the children refrain from eating the gid; rather, they are **Hashem's commandment that it not be eaten.**

The *Sefer HaChinuch* asserts, regarding the source of the mitzvah in *Torah SheBichtav*, that these words are a commandment and not a narration.[55]

Faithful to his approach, the *Sefer HaChinuch* writes regarding the mitzvah of *milah*:

> Parashat Lech Lecha contains one mitzvah, namely, the mitzvah of milah, as it says (Bereishit 17:10), "זֹאת בְּרִיתִי אֲשֶׁר תִּשְׁמְרוּ בֵּינִי וּבֵינֵיכֶם וּבֵין זַרְעֲךָ אַחֲרֶיךָ הִמּוֹל לָכֶם כָּל זָכָר — *this is My covenant that you shall uphold between Me and you and your descendants after you, every male among you shall be circumcised*," and [this mitzvah] was repeated in Parashat Tazria (Vayikra 12:3), "וּבַיּוֹם הַשְּׁמִינִי יִמּוֹל בְּשַׂר עָרְלָתוֹ — *and on the eighth day the flesh of his orlah shall be circumcised*." Many mitzvot are repeated in numerous places in the Torah, each time for a purpose, as our Chachamim, z"l, have explained them.

---

55   In our humble opinion, it may still be possible to explain the words "*lo yochlu*" as a narrative on the level of *pshat*, while the halachah explains it as a commandment, so that there is not necessarily a contradiction between the two *peirushim*.

The *Chinuch* has taken pains to distance us from the misconception that the source for the mitzvah of *milah* is from *Parashat Tazria* ("after *Matan Torah*"), and not from *Parashat Lech Lecha* ("before *Matan Torah*"). This is simply not so! *Parashat Tazria* is not "after *Matan Torah*," but rather "after *Parashat Yitro*." Similarly, *Parashat Lech Lecha* is not "before *Matan Torah*," it is simply "before *Parashat Yitro*." Both of these *parshiyot* are part of *Matan Torah*, and both were transmitted, in the words of the Ramban in his introduction to *Bereishit*, "from Hashem's 'mouth' to Moshe's ear." It is indeed true that the background to *Parashat Lech Lecha* is historical in nature, and therefore we could not learn the mitzvah of *milah* from the (narrative) *pasuk*, "וַיָּמָל אֶת בְּשַׂר עָרְלָתָם — *and he [Avraham] circumcised the flesh of their orlah*." Nevertheless, an expression of *tzivui* will obligate, even if the background is one of *sippur*, in the same way that an expression of *sippur* within a halachic section of the Torah (for example, "וַיַּעֲלוּ עֹלֹת — *and they offered burnt offerings*," at the end of *Parashat Mishpatim*, 24:5) does not result in a mitzvah. We should note that there are numerous *pesukim* in that section of *Parashat Lech Lecha* that contain commands regarding *milah*. The *Sefer HaChinuch* clearly chose *pasuk* 10 as his source, since it is the first *pasuk* in that section that contains a commandment.

Building the *Beit HaMikdash*

Based on this principle, the **Kesef Mishneh** similarly explains why the **Rambam** (Hilchot Beit HaBechirah 1:1) derived the mitzvah of building the *Beit HaMikdash* from the *pasuk* "וְעָשׂוּ לִי מִקְדָּשׁ — **they shall make** Me a Mikdash" (*Shemot* 25:8), which was written within the context of the making the Mishkan in the desert, and not from the *pasuk* "וְהָיָה הַמָּקוֹם אֲשֶׁר יִבְחַר ה' אֱלֹהֵיכֶם בּוֹ לְשַׁכֵּן שְׁמוֹ שָׁם — *it shall be the place that Hashem your God shall choose to cause His Name to dwell there*" (*Devarim* 12:11), which refers explicitly to the *Beit HaMikdash* in Eretz Yisrael. In fact, the *Sefer Mitzvot HaGadol* mentions this second *pasuk* as the source for this particular mitzvah! However, the Rambam did not quote the *pasuk* in *Devarim,* since it is not written in the form of a commandment but rather describes the *Beit HaMikdash* as the setting for the bringing of *korbanot*. Rambam quotes the *pasuk* in *Shemot*, which is stated as a commandment.[56]

A similar idea is found in the *peirush* of the **Ritva** to *Masechet Yoma* (24b), explaining how the Gemara states that lighting the Menorah is not considered an *Avodah* of the Mikdash, and even a non-Kohen is qualified to light. This seems difficult in light of what is said clearly in the *pasuk* "דַּבֵּר אֶל אַהֲרֹן וְאָמַרְתָּ אֵלָיו בְּהַעֲלֹתְךָ אֶת הַנֵּרֹת — *speak to* **Aharon**, *and say to him, 'when you kindle the lights'*"!

To this the Ritva answers:

> *It is possible to suggest that it is for this reason the Torah did not express this as a **commandment**, i.e., "Speak to Aharon and **he will** kindle the lights," in order to teach us that it is not an avodah for which a non-Kohen would incur liability if he performed it.*

We find this idea discussed among the Acharonim as well. Thus, for example, **R' Meir Simcha HaKohen of Dvinsk**, author of the **Meshech Chochmah** (*Shemot* 40:2), writes that the correct source for the halachah that building the *Beit HaMikdash* must be done by day and not by night (*Masechet Shevuot* 15b) is the *pasuk* "בְּיוֹם הַחֹדֶשׁ הָרִאשׁוֹן... תָּקִים אֶת מִשְׁכַּן אֹהֶל מוֹעֵד — *on the* **day** *of the first month... you shall set up the Mishkan*" (*Shemot* ibid.) and not the *pasuk* "וּבְיוֹם הָקִים אֶת הַמִּשְׁכָּן — *and on the* **day** *the Mishkan was set up*" (*Bamidbar* 9:15), as the first *pasuk* is written in the form of *tzivui*, while the second *pasuk* is written in the form of *sippur*.

From all these examples we can see clearly that the way the Torah chooses to write something determines whether it obligates on a *d'Oraita* level. *Pesukim* are deemed to be mitzvot if they are written as commandments.

Part II: In Halichot[57]

THE DIFFERENCE BETWEEN *lashon tzivui* and *lashon sippur* is not only significant with regards to halachah. In *Parashat Lech Lecha*, the **Meshech Chochmah** discusses this principle within the context of Hashem's words to Avraham in the *Brit Bein HaBetarim* (15:13–14):

וַיֹּאמֶר לְאַבְרָם יָדֹעַ תֵּדַע כִּי גֵר יִהְיֶה זַרְעֲךָ בְּאֶרֶץ לֹא לָהֶם וַעֲבָדוּם
וְעִנּוּ אֹתָם אַרְבַּע מֵאוֹת שָׁנָה: וְגַם אֶת הַגּוֹי אֲשֶׁר יַעֲבֹדוּ דָּן אָנֹכִי
וְאַחֲרֵי כֵן יֵצְאוּ בִּרְכֻשׁ גָּדוֹל:

He said to Avram, "Know that your descendants will be
strangers in a land that is not their own, and they will
serve them; and they will persecute them for four hundred
years. And also the nation that they will serve, I will judge,
and afterwards they will leave with great wealth."

Why Were the Mitzrim Punished?

The major question that is raised here is, how can Hashem punish the Mitzrim for what they did to Bnei Yisrael when He already decreed, as far back as the time of Avraham Avinu, that these events will come to pass? We should emphasize that we are not dealing here solely with Hashem's **knowledge** of the event in advance,[58] but with His **transmitting this knowledge** to a human being, which means that now a person knows in advance what another person will choose in the future!

---

57   [The Rav used the term "*halichot*" to refer to the non-halachic parts of Torah that are there to teach us correct behavior. He preferred this term to "*sippur*," which has a somewhat lighter connotation.]

58   [In which case we could say — as the Rambam there does — that since Hashem's knowledge is ultimately unknowable to us, we cannot meaningfully pose a contradiction between that knowledge and a person's free will.]

The Rambam's Approach — a Decree on the Nation Leaves Free Will for the Individual

The resolution of this major question is the subject of a famous *machloket* between two of the great *Rishonim*, the Rambam and the Ramban.

The **Rambam** writes in the **Mishneh Torah** (*Hilchot Teshuvah*, chapters 5 and 6):

> *Every individual has the ability to incline himself toward a path of good and be a tzaddik, and if he wants to incline himself toward a path of evil and be a rasha, he can do so... this is a major principle and is the foundation of Torah and mitzvot... There are a number of pesukim in the Torah and Nevi'im that would seem to contradict this principle...it is written, "And they will serve them; and they will persecute them," which means Hashem is decreeing that the Mitzrim will do evil!*

The Rambam continues, and answers this question:

> *Each individual who afflicted and persecuted Israel, had he not wished to persecute that person, he could have chosen not to, for the decree did not involve any **specific person**, rather, that Avraham's descendants would be persecuted [**generally**] in a land that is not theirs.*

The Ramban's Approach — Staying within the Boundaries of the Decree

This position of the Rambam is disputed by the **Ramban** (*Bereishit* 15:14), who writes:

> *His approach does not seem to me to be correct, for even had Hashem decreed that "one of the nations should persecute them in such and such a manner," and a nation should*

*then proceed to fulfill Hashem's decree, **they have merited performing a mitzvah**! Indeed, what reason is there in his (Rambam's) words? When a king decrees that people of a certain region should perform a certain act, one who is lax and passes it on to others to do is negligent and sins against his soul, whereas one who does this act will find favor with the king. This should certainly be the case here where the pasuk states "And the nation that they will serve," which implies that they will serve the entire nation...rather, the reason [they were punished] is as I have written.*

The "reason" the Ramban refers to for the Mitzrim being punished is one he has written earlier on in that section:

*They were evil **in excess of the decree**, for they threw their sons into the Nile [something which is not included in "and they will persecute them"], and they embittered their lives and tried to wipe out their name [again, in excess of that which was decreed]. And this is the meaning of the words "דָּן*
*אָנֹכִי — I will **judge** them," meaning, I will call them to judgment[59] whether or not they acted in accordance with that which was decreed concerning them,[60] or were excessively evil toward them.[61]*

Thus we have before us a most fundamental *machloket* between the Rambam and the Ramban in how to understand this *sugya* in the Torah.

The *Meshech Chochmah* — *Tzivui* vs. *Sippur*

The approach taken by the *Meshech Chochmah* in this *sugya* is to

---

59   I.e., the word "דָּן" here does not refer to punishing them but literally to judging them.

60   In which case they would be considered "partners" with Hashem in the performance of a mitzvah!

61   In which case they would be punished, in accordance with the judgment of "דָּן אָנֹכִי."

defend the position of the Rambam, responding to the question that was raised by the Ramban (*pasuk* 13, s.v. *va'avadum*):

> *The Ramban writes at length that he does not accept the view of the Rambam, and indeed his words would have been appropriate had the pasuk been stated as a* **tzivui** *(commandment) that another nation would enslave them.*[62] *However, here it was said in the form of* **sippur** *(narration), "and they will serve them; and they will persecute them,"*[63] *and that is why they were punished,*[64] *for this is something Bnei Noach are forbidden to do according to law, for they have been commanded regarding dinim,*[65] *especially as they also thereby displayed ungratefulness,*[66] *for they had become wealthy through Yosef and had learned wisdom from him.*[67]

This, then, according to the *Meshech Chochmah*, is the explanation of the Rambam's position. Bnei Noach have a standing obligation to act in accordance with the dictates of *dinim*. Additionally, *hakarat hatov* obligates a Ben Noach as a mitzvah that is included in the mitzvah of *dinim* of the seven mitzvot of Bnei Noach. This is

---

62 For then it would indeed have been a decree, and anyone who chose to fulfill it would be performing a mitzvah.

63 Which means Hashem is addressing Avraham about what will happen and not addressing the nations, telling them that they should make it happen.

64 For persecuting Bnei Yisrael where there was no mitzvah (decree) to do so.

65 As one of the seven *mitzvot* of Bnei Noach (Rambam, *Hilchot Melachim* 9:1). Subjugating an entire nation for no justifiable reason is certainly a violation of this mitzvah, for it is *gezel* of the person, which would be forbidden by virtue of a *kal vachomer* from the *issur* of stealing his money!

66 This is similar to what the Ramban writes in *Devarim* 23:5, that Amon and Moav were barred from marrying into Bnei Yisrael since they were the beneficiaries of *chessed* from Avraham and were therefore **obligated** to deal kindly with Bnei Yisrael. We see here that the mitzvah of *dinim* for Bnei Noach incorporates the mitzvah of *hakarat hatov* and of not acting in an ungrateful manner.

67 As Pharaoh says, "אֵין נָבוֹן וְחָכָם כָּמוֹךָ אַתָּה תִּהְיֶה עַל בֵּיתִי — *there is none more wise or discerning than you; you shall oversee my household*" (*Bereishit* 41:39–40), yet subsequently, "לֹא יָדַע אֶת יוֹסֵף — *he [Pharaoh] did not recognize Yosef*" (*Shemot* 1:8).

something we find at the very beginning of human history, where Adam said "הָאִשָּׁה אֲשֶׁר נָתַתָּה עִמָּדִי — *the woman that You gave to me*" (*Bereishit* 3:12), upon which Rashi comments, "כָּאן כָּפַר בַּטּוֹבָה — *here he refused to acknowledge kindness*." As long as there is no explicit **commandment** that negates this mitzvah, it will be operative and obligatory in every situation. Hashem's words **to** Avraham **about** the nations were said in the form of a narration, not a commandment. Therefore, the mitzvah of *hakarat hatov*, as part of the mitzvot of Bnei Noach, forbids any act of aggression of the Mitzrim toward Bnei Yisrael in Mitzrayim.

Thus, we find that the distinction between *tzivui* and *sippur* is one that has ramifications not only in the sections of the Torah that relate to *halachot*, but also in those sections that relate to *halichot*!

Ma'amar Six

DIBUR YASHIR –
DIRECT (QUOTED) SPEECH IN THE TORAH

Part I: Eliezer — Eved or Ish?

A CENTRAL QUESTION discussed among the *mefarshim* regarding the Torah's narration of Eliezer's journey to find a wife for Yitzchak relates to the constantly changing usage of the terms "*eved*" and "*ish*" in reference to Eliezer. The guiding principle among the *mefarshim* is that when Eliezer is acting purely as Avraham's *shaliach* (emissary), as is befitting, without any "*chiddushim*" of his own, he is called an "*eved*," since an *eved* has no wish other than that of his master. However, when he begins to add his own ideas (even in the interests of succeeding in his mission), then he is called "*ish*," having departed from the category of an *eved* who acts strictly in accordance with his master's instructions.

The *mefarshim* demonstrate how each of the changes Eliezer introduced was done solely for the purpose of ensuring the success of the mission. This was despite the fact that he knew that if his mission should fail, it was he — Eliezer — who would stand to gain, for Chazal tell us (*Bereishit Rabbah* 59:12) Eliezer had a daughter who he hoped would be eligible to marry Yitzchak if no one suitable could be found from among Avraham's family. In setting these considerations aside, Eliezer is the epitome of *eved ne'eman* — faithful servant to Avraham.

With this in mind, let us discuss a shift in reference from "*eved*" to "*ish*" toward the end of the story.

The Way to Phrase a Question

When the *pasuk* describes Rivkah going with Eliezer, Avraham's *shaliach*, we would have expected him to be referred to as "*eved*," for we are dealing with the successful completion of his *shlichut*. Thus, **Rabbeinu Bachye** is troubled by the words of Rivkah's family when they ask her (*Bereishit* 24:58), "הֲתֵלְכִי עִם הָאִישׁ הַזֶּה — *will you go with this* **man**?" Why is Eliezer called an *ish* in this *pasuk*?

Rabbeinu Bachye answers:

> *For these are not* **the words of the Torah***; rather, they are* **the words of her brother and mother,** *and it is inconceivable that they would ask "Will you go with this* eved*?" for that is not in keeping with the ways of mussar*[68] *and is disrespectful to Rivkah.*[69]

Here we meet the fundamental principle of direct speech in the Torah, whose parameters and guidelines differ from when the Torah itself is talking.[70]

An Alternative Suggestion — Casting Aspersions

Elsewhere,[71] we discussed that sometimes, what is phrased as a question is not so much an inquiry but more of a challenge or rhetorical

---

68   [I.e., it is disrespectful to Eliezer to refer to him as an *eved* in his presence.]

69   [To imply that they would be prepared to send her accompanied only by an *eved*.]

70   In the *sefer Kedushat Peshuto Shel Mikra*, this principle is discussed in *Parshiot Toldot, Vayeitzei, Vayishlach, Vayeishev, Mikeitz,* and *Shemot.*

71   *Kedushat Peshuto Shel Mikra, Parashat Lech Lecha.*

question. In light of this, perhaps we can suggest interpreting her brother and mother's words, "Will you go with this *ish*?!" as being posed incredulously; how do you know that this man is indeed an *eved* of Avraham? Perhaps he is nothing of the sort! How are you prepared to go with this person, who is an *ish* that we have never met before? All this was part of their attempt to dissuade her from joining Avraham's household, similar to their other request (*pasuk* 55), "תֵּשֵׁב הַנַּעֲרָה אִתָּנוּ יָמִים אוֹ עָשׂוֹר אַחַר תֵּלֵךְ — *let the girl stay with us for a year or ten months.*" At any rate, whether their intention was to display courtesy or to raise suspicion, the correct choice of word for them in that sentence was "*ish*," and that is how the Torah presents it.

Part II: Reconciling Objective Truth with Subjective Feeling

SO FAR, WE have learned that direct (quoted) speech cannot be understood in exactly the same way as the Torah's "own" words. A deeper level of the principle at work here is that direct speech contains two elements which, at first glance, are self-contradictory. On the one hand, direct speech is personal and reflects a subjective feeling. On the other hand, everything that is written in the Torah, "from Hashem's 'mouth' to Moshe's ear,"[72] is absolute, objective truth!

The resolution of this contradiction is the following: direct speech in the Torah reflects the absolute truth regarding the subjective feeling of the person. It does not, however, necessarily mean that Hashem agrees with that feeling. Thus, for example, we find that Elisha, upon seeing his *Rebbe*, Eliyahu, ascend to heaven, called out (*Melachim* II, 2:14), "אַיֵּה ה' אֱלֹהֵי אֵלִיָּהוּ— *where is Hashem the God of Eliyahu?*" Elisha felt that is was appropriate to use the term "אֱלֹקֵי" with regards to Eliyahu, and not just in relation to the *Avot*. As we know, Hashem "*paskened*" differently in this matter, for we may only

---

72   Ramban's introduction to his *peirush* on the Torah.

use the term "אֱלֹקַי" with regards to the *Avot*. As R' Eliyahu Mizrachi puts it (*Bereishit* 12:3), "He [Elisha] said it of his own understanding." In other words, this was Elisha's personal exclamation and not an objective assessment.

The Brothers' Admission of Guilt — אֲבָל אֲשֵׁמִים אֲנַחְנוּ

In *Parashat Mikeitz*, the Torah presents the reaction of the brothers to the baffling and distressing events that befell them in Mitzrayim. They are accused of being spies, and Shimon is being held hostage until they bring Binyamin down to Mitzrayim. Even though twenty years had passed since they sold Yosef, his sale still remains firmly in their consciousness, either because their father has been in mourning this entire time, or (according to Rashi, based on Chazal) because they had decided to take advantage of their trip to Mitzrayim to also search for Yosef and bring him back to his father. It should come as no surprise, therefore, that when one of them is placed in jail and they are commanded to bring their younger brother from home, they begin to look for the cause of this distressing situation. They surely noticed that nothing even remotely similar happened to any of the other people who came to Mitzrayim to buy food! The brothers say (*Bereishit* 42:21):

אֲבָל אֲשֵׁמִים אֲנַחְנוּ עַל אָחִינוּ אֲשֶׁר רָאִינוּ צָרַת נַפְשׁוֹ בְּהִתְחַנְנוֹ
אֵלֵינוּ וְלֹא שָׁמָעְנוּ עַל כֵּן בָּאָה אֵלֵינוּ הַצָּרָה הַזֹּאת:

*Indeed, we are guilty concerning our brother, for we saw his
soul's anguish when he beseeched us and we did not listen;
therefore, this trouble has come upon us.*

The Brothers' Perspective

In the brothers' words, we find a cause ("we are guilty") and an effect ("therefore"). Everything is understood as happening מדה כנגד מדה, measure for measure. The *Seforno* (s.v. *be'hitchaneno*) explains the brothers' thought process during their time of distress:

"We were cruel to our brother even though we judged him to be a rodef;[73] nonetheless, we should have had compassion on him when he beseeched us. [Therefore], corresponding to our middah of cruelty, this man is now being cruel to us."

We see here clearly that the brothers admit that they are guilty. However, at the same time, they are convinced that they acted correctly in terms of absolute justice! They are guilty only insomuch as they did not act *lifnim mishurat hadin* — beyond the letter of the law. On what basis did they feel their *din* was correct? Earlier on (*Bereishit* 37:18, s.v. *vayitnaklu*), the **Seforno** explains:

> *They felt in their hearts that Yosef was plotting to kill them and that he was approaching them not to seek out their welfare, but to find some pretext for condemning them, or causing them to sin, in order that either their father should curse them, or that Hashem would punish them, leaving him alone as blessed among the sons. Here [the Torah] is informing us what caused them to act the way they did; given that they were all tzaddikim gemurim, how could they decide together to kill their brother or to sell him? For they imagined within their heart and thought that Yosef was seeking to take their souls, and the Torah tells us (Sanhedrin 72a), "when someone comes to kill you — kill him first."*

We have before us a unique situation involving the *Shevatim*, all of whom were *"tzaddikim gemurim."* On the one hand, they acknowledge their guilt, for how else could they explain the difficult circumstances in which they find themselves? (It is also clear to them that, barring the sale of Yosef, they have no other significant wrongdoing.) And yet, we see that even here they do not express their regret over the **actual sale**, for in that regard they felt that they were correct. The

---

73   As the *Seforno* explains elsewhere, see next paragraph.

only thing they feel that they did wrong was that they did not act **lifnim mishurat hadin** and have compassion on Yosef when he cried out to them.

In Their Words

This brings us to the question of direct speech. On the one hand, their words, "Indeed we are guilty... when he beseeched us and we did not listen," reflect the absolute Torah truth — regarding what the brothers thought! This does not necessarily mean that Hashem agrees with them. It is quite possible that in terms of *Beit Din Shel Maalah* they are "guilty" for having judged Yosef as a *rodef*! If this is the case, then the entire sale was wrong, not merely on the level of *lifnim mishurat hadin*, but on the level of *din* itself! It is easier for a person to see himself as "guilty" in terms of not going *lifnim mishurat hadin* than to see himself as guilty on the level of *din* itself. Even if one is forced to admit that he is "not *b'seder*," it is still difficult to see oneself as a "*rasha*," but not as difficult to see oneself as "not a *tzaddik*."

The *Seforno's* approach, that the brothers saw Yosef as a *rodef* and therefore felt that they were acting out of self-defense, is based on his understanding of (*Bereishit* 37:18) "וַיִּתְנַכְּלוּ אֹתוֹ לַהֲמִיתוֹ." The root of the word "וַיִּתְנַכְּלוּ" is "נכל," which means "plotting." Here, the word is used in the *hitpa'el* (reflexive) form, which represents what **the brothers thought** about Yosef ("אֹתוֹ"), namely, that he was plotting to kill them ("לַהֲמִיתוֹ").[74] Here, too, we have the Torah's testimony regarding what the brothers felt, but nowhere do we find **the Torah itself** saying that Yosef was plotting to kill them. This brings us back once again to their words later on of "אֲבָל אֲשֵׁמִים אֲנַחְנוּ," where the Torah tells us in which respect they thought they were guilty. Had the Torah written, "Yosef beseeched them at the time of his soul's distress, and they did not listen and were guilty," this would have constituted the testimony of the Torah that their sin was on the level

---

74 We note that on a *pshat* level, the usage of the singular form — להמיתו — is difficult if the reference is to him trying to kill **them**.

of *lifnim mishurat hadin*. And yet, we find no mention whatsoever of Yosef's entreaties to the brothers in the *perek* (*Bereishit* 37) that describes the actual sale! This element of the story is only mentioned much later on, and even then, only through the quoted words of those who were involved.

Part III: Learning Halachah D'Oraita from Direct Speech

WE HAVE SEEN that the parameters of direct speech are different from those of the Torah's own words. Direct speech has a personal, subjective element, so that when the Torah quotes someone's words, it is expressing the absolute objective truth regarding the personal, subjective feelings of the person it is quoting. It is important to realize that this distinction has implications not only for the narrative (*halichuti*) sections of Torah, but for halachah as well. The halachah will relate differently to words the Torah quotes from people than it does to the words of the Torah "itself."

Defining Halachic Terms — Meat and Milk

In *Parashat Toldot*, as Rivkah prepares Yaakov to receive the *berachot* from Yitzchak, the *pasuk* says (*Bereishit* 27:16):

וְאֵת עֹרֹת גְּדָיֵי הָעִזִּים הִלְבִּישָׁה עַל יָדָיו וְעַל חֶלְקַת צַוָּארָיו:

She put the goatskins on his arms and the smooth part of his neck.

The Gemara (*Chullin* 113b) derives a halachah from this *pasuk*:

מדפריש "גדי עזים", שמע מינה כאן גדי עזים, הא כל מקום
שנאמר "גדי" סתם, אפילו פרה ורחל במשמע.

From the fact that [the Torah] specified that these animals were "gedayei izim — goat-kids," we can infer that here they were goats, but when the Torah uses the word "gedi" by itself, it can refer even to a [kid of a] cow or a sheep.

The *Torah Temimah* explains:

*This has practical implications regarding the issur of "*לֹא *תְבַשֵּׁל גְּדִי בַּחֲלֵב אִמּוֹ* — you shall not cook a kid in its mother's milk" and teaches us that this applies not only to the milk of a goat, but also to that of a cow or sheep.*

*We may ask, why did the Gemara bring this pasuk, and not the earlier pasuk (9) that says "*לֶךְ נָא אֶל הַצֹּאן וְקַח לִי מִשָּׁם שְׁנֵי גְּדָיֵי עִזִּים *— go to the flock and there take for me two goat-kids"? Similarly, the Gemara quoted another pasuk regarding this matter in Parashat Vayeishev (38:20), "*וַיִּשְׁלַח יְהוּדָה אֶת גְּדִי הָעִזִּים *— Yehudah sent the goat-kid," but did not quote the earlier pasuk (17), "*וַיֹּאמֶר אָנֹכִי אֲשַׁלַּח גְּדִי עִזִּים *— he said, I will send a goat-kid" — is this not something astonishing?*[75]

*However, in my opinion, it is clear that the Gemara wanted to adduce a proof from **the words of the Torah** itself and not from the words of a person [direct speech], even though they are written in the Torah. Therefore, the Gemara does not quote from the earlier pesukim, for they are the spoken words of Rivkah and Yehudah, which is not the case in the later pesukim, where they are the words of the Torah itself.*

We see here the full force of the idea of direct speech in the Torah. Not only do we not learn a *d'Oraita* halachic *obligation* from direct speech, we do not even learn from it the *definition* of a word in the Torah, where that definition will have halachic consequences. Therefore, the Gemara preferred to bring a *pasuk* in which we see "the words of the Torah itself," even if that *pasuk* is later, rather than the words of someone speaking in the *pasuk*.

---

75 For it is the way of the Gemara to quote the first *pasuk* from which we can derive any given principle.

Kedushah and Halachah

We should stress clearly that in terms of *kedushah* there is no difference between the words "וַיֹּאמֶר אָנֹכִי אֲשַׁלַּח גְּדִי עִזִּים" and the words "אָנֹכִי ה' אֱלֹהֶיךָ." We are not dealing here with the *kedushah* of the words, but with their level of objective halachic potency. The Rambam has already taught us that there is no difference between the *kedushah* of the three words "אָנֹכִי ה' אֱלֹהֶיךָ" and the three words "וְתִמְנַע הָיְתָה פִילֶגֶשׁ." If one letter were to be missing from either of these phrases, the *Sefer Torah* would be *pasul*, for the absence of even one letter affects the *shleimut* — completeness of the Torah. However, regarding the level at which these words will create an actual halachic obligation, there is a great difference.

When we use the term "level of obligation" we are referring to the words of the *pasuk* as being halachically obligating. This is similar to the principle that we do not derive a *halachah d'Oraita* from the Torah's narratives ("*derech sippur*"). When the *pasuk* says (*Bereishit* 19:27), "וַיַּשְׁכֵּם אַבְרָהָם בַּבֹּקֶר אֶל הַמָּקוֹם אֲשֶׁר עָמַד שָׁם אֶת פְּנֵי ה'" — *Avraham arose early in the morning and went to the place where he stood before Hashem,*" we derive from there a *din d'rabanan* that one should stand before Hashem (in *tefillah*) each morning. Had the *pasuk* instead said, "Hashem said to Avraham, 'Arise in the morning and stand there before me,'" it would have constituted a *mitzvah d'Oraita* exactly as when Hashem tells Avraham to perform the mitzvah of *milah*. The same distinction holds true regarding the halachic status of direct speech quoted in the Torah.

As we discussed in the previous *ma'amar*, direct speech represents the Torah's objective presentation of what the person subjectively thought or said. The thoughts and deeds of a person, even one as great as one of the *Avot*, do not halachically obligate Am Yisrael unless Hashem commands that we act in a similar way to that person. As long as the Torah is not *commanding* but merely *narrating*, this can express Hashem's Will (which Chazal can translate into a halachah that obligates **on a *d'rabanan* level**) but not an obligation on the level of *d'Oraita*.

Ma'amar Seven

DERACHEHA DARCHEI NOAM

WE LEARN A major principle regarding Torah from Shlomo HaMelech (*Mishlei* 3:17), namely, that "דְּרָכֶיהָ דַרְכֵי נֹעַם — *its ways are ways of pleasantness.*" This principle finds expression in every area of learning and understanding Torah. Let's begin by seeing how "*deracheha darchei noam*" affects *signon hakatuv* — the way the Torah expresses itself.

The Sequence of *Tzora'at*

Rabbeinu Bachye (*Vayikra* 14:54–56) writes:

> The **tradition received by Chazal** (*Midrash Tanchuma Metzora* section 4) describes the order of the types of tzora'at as they occur **in actuality**. Initially, Hashem afflicts the person's **house** so that his heart shall be contrite and he may examine his ways and do teshuvah. If he did teshuvah — well and good. If not, He afflicts his **clothes**. If he did teshuvah — well and good. If not, He afflicts the **body** itself. Nonetheless, that is not the order in which these afflictions appear in the parshiyot [sections], for the first parashah discusses "נֶגַע צָרַעַת

82

כִּי תִהְיֶה בְאָדָם — *an affliction of tzora'at if it should be in **a per-**
son*"[76] *(13:9), after that comes* "וְהַבֶּגֶד כִּי יִהְיֶה בוֹ נֶגַע צָרַעַת — *if
a **garment** should have an affliction of tzora'at" (pasuk 47),
and the final parashah is* "וְנָתַתִּי נֶגַע צָרַעַת בְּבֵית אֶרֶץ אֲחֻזַּתְכֶם —
*and I will place a tzora'at affliction upon a **house** in the land
of your possession" (14:34)!*[77]
*The reason why the Torah chose this way — to first mention
tzora'at of the body, then of clothing, and finally of houses, is
because "deracheha darchei noam," all the Torah's ways are
ways of pleasantness. Therefore, it ordered them in a way
that the afflictions should not proceed in increasing levels
of suffering, as is in fact the case,*[78] *but rather in decreasing
levels of suffering, as indicated by the order of the parshiyot.*

In other words, the principle of *"darchei noam"* finds expression in
the way in which the afflictions are presented in the *pasuk*, as going
from more severe to less severe (which is a "positive approach"),
and not, *chas v'shalom*, from less severe to more severe. We thus see
that the parameters of *peshuto shel mikra* may sometimes be entirely
different from those of the halachic reality, as known to us through
kabbalat Rabboteinu z"l.

Bringing the Flood

The basic idea of **Rabbeinu Bachye** regarding the impact of *"deracheha darchei noam"* on *signon hakatuv* can been seen earlier on in his
comments on the *parashah* of the *Mabul (Bereishit 7:11, s.v. nivke'u)*:

It is for this reason the Torah does not write "**Hashem** brought
the Mabul on the earth for forty days and forty nights,"
for it did not wish to mention Hashem's Name explicitly in

---

76   [I.e., his body.]
77   So that the order in the *pasuk* is the exact opposite of the order transmitted to us through
     kabbalat Chazal.
78   Namely, in actuality, as per *kabbalat Chazal.*

connection with calamity,[79] *although the matter is known that it is He who brought the Mabul, as He already said (6:17),* "וְאֲנִי הִנְנִי מֵבִיא— *and behold, I will bring,"* nonetheless, the Torah, whose "ways are ways of pleasantness" (deracheha darchei noam) judged it appropriate to refer to Hashem here in an indirect manner and not mention Him explicitly. *Similarly, it says (7:23),* "וַיִּמַח אֶת כָּל הַיְקוּם — *He wiped out all existence" and does not say "Hashem wiped out all existence." Additionally, we find that when He punished Adam and Chavah, the pasuk stated nonspecifically,* "אֶל הָאִשָּׁה אָמַר — *to the woman He said" (3:16),* "וּלְאָדָם אָמַר — *and to Adam He said" (3:17) and did not mention Hashem's Name when they were being cursed. However, when it comes to the Attribute of Mercy, Hashem's Name is mentioned explicitly.*[80]

Light and Darkness

Based on this idea, Rabbeinu Bachye also explains why in *Parashat Bereishit* (1:5) the Torah says, "וַיִּקְרָא אֱלֹהִים לָאוֹר יוֹם וְלַחֹשֶׁךְ קָרָא לָיְלָה — *Hashem called the light 'Day,' and the darkness He called 'Night,'"* again mentioning Hashem's Name only in connection with light, so that it should only be associated with positive things.

Indeed, this idea mentioned by Rabbeinu Bachye that "Hashem does not associate His name with evil" is enunciated by Chazal in the Midrash (*Bereishit Rabbah* 3:8). From here we see that Chazal themselves had already identified and expressed the concept that Rabbeinu Bachye subsequently discussed at length.

Darchei Noam in the Realm of Halachah

From the *beit midrash* of the *Rishonim*, we now turn to the *Gedolei Ha'Acharonim* to see how the concept of "*darchei noam*" affects the

---

79   See *Bereishit Rabbah* 3:8, "Hashem does not attach His name to evil, only to good."

80   Rabbeinu Bachye then proceeds to describe how, when it comes to matters of mercy and salvation, Hashem's Name is mentioned explicitly.

way the halachah itself is written in the Torah. Let us begin with the
Meshech Chochmah (*Vayikra* 2:14, s.v. *ve'im takriv*):

> With regards to the korban ha'omer, the Torah did not write
> that the remnant of the korban should be eaten by Aharon and
> his sons, as it did with other korbanot minchah.[81] Similarly,
> this [the Kohanim eating the remnant of the korban] is not
> mentioned with regards to the korban of the Sotah;[82] rather,
> the Gemara Bavli (Menachot 72b) and Yerushalmi (Sotah,
> perek 3) derive this from derashot. The reason **why the
> Torah did not write this explicitly** is because barley [from
> which the korban ha'omer and korban sotah are brought] is
> animal food, and therefore the Torah did not wish to state
> that Aharon and his sons should share in eating them, for
> this is not in keeping with their honor. Hashem has more
> consideration for the honor of His creations than He does for
> the honor of the Mizbey'ach![83]

Yibum and *Chalitzah*

Based on this principle of "*darchei noam*," we may suggest an explanation concerning a shift in phraseology within the *parashah* of
yibum. In the event of *chalitzah*, the Torah requires the woman to say
about her deceased husband's brother, "לֹא אָבָה יַבְּמִי — *he does not consent to perform yibum with me*" (Devarim 25:7), whereas, in the very
next *pasuk*, the brother is required to say "לֹא חָפַצְתִּי לְקַחְתָּהּ — *I do not
wish to marry her*" (ibid., pasuk 8). The change in wording between
these two *pesukim* is quite peculiar. Why don't they both use either
the term "אבה," or the term "חפץ"? Also, why does she say that he does
not wish "יַבְּמִי — to perform *yibum* with me," while he says he does
not wish "לְקַחְתָּהּ — to marry her"?

---

81 See e.g., *Vayikra* 2:3.
82 See *Bamidbar perek* 5.
83 For the Torah does openly write that these barley *korbanot* are offered on the *Mizbey'ach*.

We would like to suggest that the Torah is demonstrating special sensitivity with these shifts in nuance, both to the man and to the woman:

- The term "חפץ" reflects a desire or attraction that is not intellectual in nature, but emotional, whereas "אבה" is a connection that is based on intellectual grounds.
- Additionally, the term "*lakach*" refers to the act of *kiddushin* (as in "כִּי יִקַּח אִישׁ אִשָּׁה" in *Devarim* 24:1), whereas the term "*yabam*" refers, of course, to the mitzvah of *yibum*.

With this in mind, we will understand that it would not be "*darchei noam*" to require the woman to say that this man did not find her attractive to the extent that he would like to marry her. Therefore, all she has to say is that he does not wish to perform the mitzvah of *yibum* with her. On the other hand, it is also not in keeping with "*darchei noam*" to require the man to say that he is not prepared to fulfill a mitzvah of the Torah. Instead, he merely says that he does not feel sufficiently attracted on an emotional level to take this woman as his wife, which does not reflect badly on anyone involved.

Therefore, when the Torah itself describes the situation, it also says "וְאִם לֹא יַחְפֹּץ הָאִישׁ לָקַחַת אֶת יְבִמְתּוֹ" — *and if the man does not wish to marry his sister-in-law*"[84] and does not say "וְאִם לֹא אָבָה הָאִישׁ לְיַבֵּם" — *and if the man decides not to perform yibum.*"[85]

This, in my humble opinion, is the way to explain the terms used by the Torah in presenting the mitzvah of *yibum* based on the theme of "*darchei noam*." This is especially appropriate with this mitzvah, where the Torah itself provides an alternative (*chalitzah*) in the event that the mitzvah of *yibum* is not performed.

Naming a *Mizbey'ach*

Elsewhere, R' Meir Simcha explains the name that Yitzchak Avinu gave to one of the *mizbechot* that he built as being based on "*deracheha*

---

84   [Stating his lack of emotional attraction to her.]
85   [Which would declare a lack of commitment on his part to keeping *mitzvot*.]

darchei noam," demanding sensitivity toward the feelings of others. The **Meshech Chochmah** (*Bereishit* 26:25, s.v. *vayiven*) writes:

> *The idea of naming a mizbey'ach is in order to publicize the prophecy or miracle that led to the building of that mizbey'ach... In Yitzchak's first nevuah (pasuk 4) he was told that he and his descendants would inherit* אֶת כָּל הָאֲרָצֹת הָאֵל — *all of these lands." Nonetheless, he did not publicize this, for he was afraid that perhaps this would cause antagonism toward him from those who dwelled in these lands, and Yitzchak was not schooled in the art of warfare. Moreover, it is* **a violation of darchei mussar** *to announce his eventual takeover of the country to the very people who had acted peaceably toward him.*

It seems quite clear that the idea of "*darchei mussar*" referred to by the *Meshech Chochmah* is a very similar concept to that of "*darchei noam*." In these words of the *Meshech Chochmah* we once again encounter the idea of direct (quoted) speech, which has different parameters from those of the Torah's own words. The *pasuk* clearly stated that Hashem told Yitzchak that his descendants would inherit the entire land. However, "*darchei noam*" prevented Yitzchak from expressing this in words when he named the *mizbey'ach*.

This idea — that "*darchei mussar*" will find expression in the way people speak and may require them to phrase things differently from the way they were said to them by Hashem — can be found in the **Meiri's** Introduction to his *peirush* on *Sefer Tehillim*:

> *...Hashem said to Shmuel regarding Yishai of Beit Lechem (Shmuel I, 16:1),* "כִּי רָאִיתִי בְּבָנָיו לִי מֶלֶךְ" — *for I have seen among his sons a king for Me." Even though elsewhere he was called a "Naggid" (ruler), as when Shmuel said to Shaul (ibid., 13:14),* "בִּקֵּשׁ ה' לוֹ אִישׁ כִּלְבָבוֹ וַיְצַוֵּהוּ ה' לְנָגִיד" — *Hashem has sought out a man after His own heart and appointed*

him a ruler over His people," this was due to "derech hamus-
sar," which required that he not describe David in front of
Shaul as being greater than him.

Darchei Noam and Ta'amei HaMitzvot

Taking the discussion one step further, we should note that
"*darchei noam*" affects not only the way the Torah writes about
things, it also *expresses* itself in the reasons for mitzvot.

In his commentary to *Sefer Bereishit* (9:7, s.v. *peru u'revu*), the
Meshech Chochmah writes:

> *It is not implausible to suggest that the reason the Torah*
> *exempted women from the mitzvah of peru u'revu, and*
> *only obligated men,*[86] *is because Hashem's ways are "ways*
> *of pleasantness" (darchei noam) and do not obligate the*
> *body in something that it cannot manage. Thus, in every*
> *category where the Torah forbade something, it permit-*
> *ted a corresponding item in that category.*[87] *It is for this*
> *reason we find the Torah commands us to fast only one*
> *day a year [Yom Kippur], and [even then] exhorts and*
> *commands us to eat beforehand.*[88] *Similarly, the Torah*
> *did not withhold people from marital relations, with*
> *the exception of Moshe who, due to his exalted status,*
> *had no need for them. So too in the case of women, for*
> *whom pregnancy and childbirth can involve an element*

---

86 See *Yevamot* 64b, and Rambam *Hilchot Ishut* at the beginning of chapter 15.

87 See *Chullin* 109b; "Yalta said to Rav Nachman, 'Consider that everything the Torah has
forbidden, it has allowed an item which is similar: it forbade blood — and permitted liver; it
forbade *niddah* blood — but permitted blood of purity; it forbade the fat of animals — and
permitted the fat of beasts.'"

88 See *Berachot* 8b commenting on the *pasuk* (*Vayikra* 23:32) "וְעִנִּיתֶם אֶת נַפְשֹׁתֵיכֶם בְּתִשְׁעָה לַחֹדֶשׁ בָּעֶרֶב —
and you shall afflict your souls on the ninth of the month, in the evening,"; "Do we indeed fast on
the ninth? We fast on the tenth! Rather, it comes to tell you that anyone who eats and drinks on
the ninth is considered as if he fasted on the ninth and on the tenth."

of danger, perhaps even of death — see Tosafot Ketubot
83b, s.v. mitah shechicha[89] *— hence, the Torah did not*
impose the commandment of peru u'revu on women.

We see from these words of the *Meshech Chochmah* that "*darchei noam*" can be a determining factor in the rationale for a mitzvah, even one that is written like all other mitzvot with no explicit rationale given in the *pasuk*.

In this next paragraph, returning to the matter of *tzora'at*, we will see how the **Meshech Chochmah** uses "*darchei noam*" to explain the *pasuk al derech hapshat* in a way that is parallel to (but not in conflict with) something Chazal derived *al derech hamidrash* (Vayikra 13:3, s.v. *v'ra'a hakohen*):

There is an obvious repetition in the pasuk,[90] *see the Torat*
Kohanim there.[91] *It is possible to explain, based on Chazal,*
that the meaning of the first phrase is that he should see the
nega (affliction) and determine if it should be pronounced
tamei, i.e., if it has a sign of tumah — white hair. The second
phrase, "v'ra'ahu haKohen," means the Kohen should look
at the person *and see if it is appropriate to render him*
tamei. [For example,] if he is newly married, they allow
him the seven days of feasting; similarly, if it is a chag, he
is given all seven days of chag in order not to disrupt his joy
(Mo'ed Katan 7b), for "deracheha darchei noam." Therefore,
"v'ra'ahu" means to examine the person's situation, wheth-
er it is appropriate to render him tamei at that time. And
this is the meaning of the words later on (pasuk 14), "וּבְיוֹם

---

89   "Perhaps it is because in most cases she endangers herself during childbirth" (*Tosafot* ibid.).

90   [The *pasuk* begins with the words "וְרָאָה הַכֹּהֵן אֶת הַנֶּגַע — *and the Kohen shall see the affliction,*" and then says "וְרָאָהוּ הַכֹּהֵן — *and the Kohen shall see it.*"]

91   Chapter 2 section 8; "*v'ra'ahu* — the *nega* must be entirely visible at the same time. If it was on two sides of his nose or finger, he is not *tamei*. In other words, the *Torat Kohanim* explains the word "*v'ra'ahu*" refers to the *nega* itself. In contrast, the *Meshech Chochmah* explains that it refers to the person who is afflicted.

הֵרָאוֹת בּוֹ — *and on the day it appears within it," [from which Chazal derived that] there are days when the person is not examined. In other words, this idea of choosing not to examine the person is only affected by time, and we would not say, for example, that if his emotional constitution required that he stay in other people's company and other such considerations, that we would not examine him. Rather,*[92] *it is only the question of timing that affects when he is seen; understand this well.*

In a similar manner, the **Sefer HaChinuch** (Mitzvah 376) explains the reason for the mitzvah of a Kohen to become *tamei* for a member of his immediate family:

> *A regular Kohen, even though he is sanctified, becomes tamei for them [the seven close family members]. The reason for this, it appears, is that the kedushah of a Kohen devolves upon him naturally; it is not something that he chose to receive. Rather, he was sanctified at birth due to the kedushah of his tribe. This means that his interaction with his family is the same as anyone else's, for there is no difference between him and them except that there are times when he performs the Avodah in the Beit HaMikdash. But there are also times when he is residing in his home and enjoying the company of his friends. At times of rejoicing and feasting he will invite his friends and relatives. Therefore, he will become very emotionally attached to them, and they to him. And it is for this reason he is permitted to become tamei for them, for "deracheha darchei noam."*

---

92   This is the *chiddush* contained within the words *"v'ra'ahu hakohen,"* which the *Meshech Chochmah* explains in parallel to the *drashah* of Chazal on the words *"uv'yom hera'ot,"* namely, that the person must be examined to see if he is able to be quarantined as a *metzora* during that time.

There is a similar discussion of *"darchei noam"* and *ta'amei ham-itzvot* from the *beit midrash* of **Rabbeinu Bachye** (*Vayikra* 11:30, s.v. *v'hachomet*):

> *The Torah mentioned eight sheratzim and said (pasuk 31),*
> *"אֵלֶּה הַטְּמֵאִים לָכֶם — these shall be tamei for you," yet the*
> *snake is not counted among them. This is very strange, for*
> *it would certainly have been appropriate for the snake to be*
> *tamei and render others tamei, for he is the source of tumah*
> *and spiritual pollution, as is known from the original snake*
> *in Gan Eden. If so, why would the pesukim not include it*
> *among the sheratzim that cause tumah? However, this mat-*
> *ter is on account of the ways of the Torah, "whose pathways*
> *are peace," that it did not wish for the snake to cause tumah*
> *through contact, for if so, a person may refrain from killing a*
> *snake in order not to become tamei.*

Darchei Noam as a Factor in Determining Halachah

So far we have seen how the principle of *"deracheha darchei noam"* can affect the way the Torah writes things, as well as how it can be used to explain the reason for certain mitzvot in the Torah. We will conclude this discussion by referring to a third area that can also be "influenced" by *"deracheha darchei noam,"* which is Chazal using this principle to determine the correct interpretation of a mitzvah in the Torah! There were times when the *pasuk* could have been explained in more than one way, and Chazal invoked *"darchei noam"* and thereby established the halachah for all time. A classic example of this is the discussion that takes place in *Masechet Succah* 32a regarding identifying the *arba minim*, specifically the *lulav*:

> *The Gemara asks, "Yet perhaps the reference is to a 'kufra'*
> *(Rashi: It is similar to a palm branch, except it is only one or*
> *two years old, and the wood has not yet thickened)?*

> Said Abaye, "It is written, 'Deracheha darchei noam v'chol
> netivoteha shalom.'" (Rashi: And these [kufra branches] are
> like thistles with many thorns protruding from them that
> can lacerate the hands).

We thus see that in each of the above three areas of Torah
(halachah, *machshavah, parshanut*) the principle of "*deracheha darchei
noam*" is operative, influential, and decisive.

The *Netzach* of Torah

As we conclude this discussion, it is in place to reiterate that this
principle of "*deracheha darchei noam*" did not originate with Shlomo
HaMelech. It was something observed and formulated based on his
study of the Torah, and he urged and encouraged us to be sure to live
our own lives based on it. It should come as no surprise, therefore, to
find this principle being used in halachic discussions by the *poskim*
throughout the generations until our own times.

As a small sample, the reader is referred to the following sources:

1. *Teshuvot HaRosh, klal* 108, *siman* 10.
2. *Teshuvot Radvaz,* section 1, *siman* 413.
3. *Teshuvot HaBach Hachadashot, siman* 34.
4. *Teshuvot Binyamin Ze'ev, siman* 182, s.v. *b'ir achat.*
5. *Teshuvot Tzitz Eliezer,* volume 10, *siman* 10, s.v. *u'mah.*
6. R' Elchanan Wasserman, *Kovetz Shiurim, Bava Batra* 34b,
   se'if 153.
7. R' Ovadya Yosef, *Yabia Omer,* volume 1, *Yoreh De'ah siman* 11.

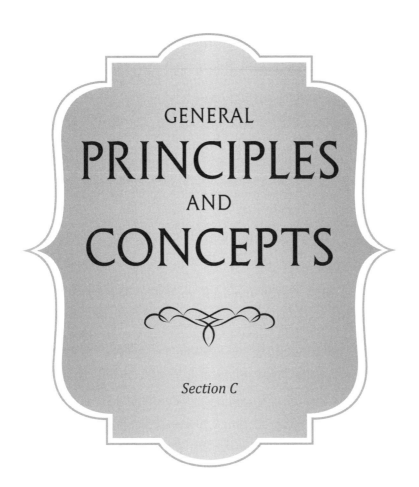

GENERAL
PRINCIPLES
AND
CONCEPTS

Section C

Ma'amar Eight

PEIRUSH CHAZAL AND KABBALAT CHAZAL

Understanding the Different Ways in Which Chazal Will Approach a *Pasuk* in the Torah

וְכוּשׁ יָלַד אֶת נִמְרֹד הוּא הֵחֵל לִהְיוֹת גִּבֹּר בָּאָרֶץ: הוּא הָיָה גִבֹּר
צַיִד לִפְנֵי ה׳ עַל כֵּן יֵאָמַר כְּנִמְרֹד גִּבּוֹר צַיִד לִפְנֵי ה׳:

*And Cush begot Nimrod; he was the first to be a mighty
man in the land. He was a mighty hunter before Hashem;
therefore, it is said, "Like Nimrod, a mighty hunter before
Hashem" (Bereishit 10:8–9).*

Lishvach or *Lignai*?

RASHI ON THIS *pasuk*, quoting Chazal, explains each and every term mentioned in the above *pasuk* in a derogatory manner (*doresh lignai*):

> **To be a mighty man** — *To cause the whole world to rebel against Hashem through the idea of the Dor HaPalagah (the Tower of Bavel).*

Before Hashem — *His intention was to anger Him (Hashem).*

Therefore it is said — *About any brazen person who causes wickedness, who knows his Creator and intends to rebel against Him, it shall be said, "This person is a 'mighty hunter' like Nimrod."*

The Ibn Ezra's Approach

Within the course of his discussion concerning Nimrod, the Ramban quotes Rashi's comments and then writes:

*And this is also Chazal's understanding [of the pasuk]. However, **R' Avraham ibn Ezra** explains the pasuk in the exact opposite manner according to the pshat — that he was a mighty man who overpowered animals and trapped them. And he explains the words "lifnei Hashem" to mean that he would build altars and offer these animals as korbanot before Hashem.*

We should note that the Ramban does not say that Rashi's explanation is *peshuto shel mikra*. On the contrary, he refers to it as "*da'at Rabboteinu* — the approach of Chazal," while it is the explanation of the Ibn Ezra that he calls "*al derech peshuto*." For this is indeed the simple meaning of the words: "*gibor tzayid*" means one who traps animals, and "*lifnei* (before) Hashem" is a seemingly positive expression [as opposed to "*neged* (against) Hashem" (*Shmuel* I, 12:3) or "*milifnei* (from before) Hashem" (*Bereishit* 4:16)].

We thus have before us a situation where Rashi (based on Chazal) is *doresh lignai* — interprets the *pesukim* as portraying Nimrod in a negative light — while the Ibn Ezra, based on *peshuto shel mikra*, is *doresh lishvach*, explaining the *pesukim* in a positive light. Seemingly, this is similar to the differing opinions we find among Chazal regarding Noach, where there are those among Chazal who are *doresh lishvach*, while others are *doresh lignai*. So too here, Chazal are *doresh*

Nimrod *lignai*, while there are those among the *Rishonim* who are *doresh lishvach*.

This license for *mefarshim* to explain the *pesukim* in a way that differs from Chazal is in keeping with the guidelines set forth by the **Ohr HaChaim HaKadosh** (*Bereishit* 1:3):

> Know that permission is given to explain the meaning of the pesukim in accordance with the ways of analysis and sound reasoning, even if earlier sources explained the pesukim in a different manner, for there are shivim panim laTorah — seventy ways of explaining the Torah. And we are not restricted from differing in our understanding of the pesukim unless it would lead to a change in the halachah. And thus you will find that even though the Amora'im do not have the authority to argue with the Tanna'im in matters of halachah, nonetheless, when it comes to the explanation of the pesukim, we find in numerous places that they will explain them in a way that differs from the way they were explained by the Tanna'im.

The Ramban's Objection — *Peirush* vs. *Kabbalah*

We should note that this principle of the possibility of even explaining *pesukim* in a way that differs from the *peirush* of Chazal, although mentioned by the *Ohr HaChaim*, is by no means his *chiddush*. It is well known to the Ramban as well as the other Rishonim.[93] This being the case, we should find ourselves quite surprised by the reaction of the **Ramban** to the Ibn Ezra's *peirush* regarding Nimrod:

> His words appear unacceptable to me, for he is portraying a rasha as a tzaddik!

---

93   See, for example, Ramban to *Bamidbar* 26:13, s.v. *l'Zerach*, regarding the families who went down to Mitzrayim.

Here we ask the following question: In what way is this discussion different from any other case where we find that there are those who are *doresh lishvach*? On the contrary, the Ibn Ezra could well respond to the Ramban, "Why are you accusing me of portraying the *rasha* as a *tzaddik*? As far as I'm concerned, you are portraying the *tzaddik* as a *rasha*!"

It is for this reason the Ramban adds the following crucial words, "כִּי רַבּוֹתֵנוּ יָדְעוּ רִשְׁעוֹ בַּקַּבָּלָה" — *for Chazal knew of his wickedness* **by means of a kabbalah (tradition)."**

This is a major principle, one which unfortunately is lost on many in our times when they come to explain the *pesukim* "in accordance with the ways of analysis and sound reasoning." A *peirush* may be legitimate even if it differs from those of earlier sources. However, this is specifically when it is not in direct conflict with a *peirush* that is based on **kabbalat Chazal.** This category of *peirush*, even though it relates to a non-halachic section of Torah, does not leave room for *peirushim* that differ from the approach **received** by Chazal. The Ramban himself expresses this distinction elsewhere, where he writes (*Bamidbar* 26:13): "*If this [explanation of Chazal] is an Aggadah (kabbalah), then we will bear the difficulty [in explaining the pasuk according to their explanation]...but if it is not kabbalat Rabboteinu, we will push away that explanation with both hands.*"

We see that the Ramban is prepared to "push away with both hands" a **peirush** of Chazal if he feels strongly that the *pshat* of the *pasuk* differs. However, when dealing with a **kabbalah** of Chazal, he is prepared to accept any difficulty that this may involve in explaining the *pesukim*.

Clarifying the Scope of the *Machloket*

Coming back to our discussion, we will presently see that the Ibn Ezra also agrees that one cannot explain a *pasuk* in a way that conflicts with a *kabbalah* of Chazal. This will lead us to a problem when it comes to his words regarding Nimrod, where he seems to have done just that! However, in his case it is possible that in his understanding,

Chazal's words regarding Nimrod were said as a *peirush* or *midrash*, not through a *kabbalah*; therefore, he allows himself to explain in a positive way that which Chazal, through the methodology of *drash*, explained negatively.

Since we are dealing with *Parashat Noach*, let us bring an example that will demonstrate to us the Ibn Ezra's full preparedness to explain the *pasuk* in accordance with *kabbalat Chazal*. In this case, the *kabbalah* may even contradict aspects of *peshuto shel mikra*, as opposed to the case of Nimrod where it is actually possible to understand the *pesukim* negatively even on a *pshat* level. We refer to the *pasuk* dealing with Avraham marrying Sarah (*Bereishit* 11:29):

שֵׁם אֵשֶׁת אַבְרָם שָׂרָי וְשֵׁם אֵשֶׁת נָחוֹר מִלְכָּה בַּת הָרָן אֲבִי מִלְכָּה
וַאֲבִי יִסְכָּה

*The name of Avram's wife was Sarai, and the name of
Nachor's wife was Milkah, the daughter of Haran, the
father of Milkah and the father of Yiskah.*

Rashi, based on Chazal, explains that "Yiskah" is actually Sarai and proceeds to quote Chazal's explanations as to why the name Yiskah is mentioned instead of Sarai. Regarding this, the **Ibn Ezra** comments:

> Our early Chachamim (kadmoneinu) said that Yiskah is
> Sarah,[94] and if it is a kabbalah — we will accept it.

The fact that the Ibn Ezra is prepared to accept the identification of Yiskah as Sarai based on *kabbalat Chazal* is significant, because the *pshat* of the *pasuk* seems to indicate otherwise, for it refers to Yiskah and Sarai as if they are two different people and refers only to Milkah as "the daughter of Haran." Nevertheless, if Chazal have a *kabbalah* in this matter, then the *pasuk* needs to be understood accordingly.

---

94   Even though this is not in accordance with the *pshat*. Moreover, why would it say "the daughter of Haran" and not "the daughters of Haran"? (*Mechokekei Yehudah*).

The Ibn Ezra's approach to *kabbalat Chazal* is echoed elsewhere, for example, in his discussion regarding which day of the week Bnei Yisrael left Mitzrayim. Based on his understanding of the *pesukim* dealing with the *Lechem HaPanim* (end of *Parashat Emor*), Ibn Ezra concludes that the day of *Yetziat Mitzrayim* could not have been later in the week than Wednesday. However, the Ibn Ezra is aware that the Gemara states that they left on a Thursday.[95] In response to this he writes:

> *If it is a kabbalah — we will accept it. But if it is based on reason — they left before Thursday.*

Here again, we see that while on the one hand the Ibn Ezra is prepared to explain *pesukim* in a way that differs from a *peirush* ("based on reason") of Chazal, he is equally prepared to retract his explanation if the words of Chazal are based on a *kabbalah*. Moreover, we can see from this case that the question as to whether or not any given explanation of Chazal is indeed a *peirush* or perhaps a *kabbalah* is itself not always clear, and the Ibn Ezra takes both possibilities into account.

What emerges from this is that the *machloket* between the Ibn Ezra and the Ramban regarding Nimrod is not so much one of **principle**, i.e., whether one may explain something contrary to a *kabbalah* of Chazal, but rather one of **application**, with the question being, are we to understand that Chazal's words regarding Nimrod were in fact based on a *kabbalah*?

Kabbalah of Facts vs. Kabbalah of a Peirush

Taking this discussion one step further, we will note that even in a case where there is a *kabbalah* from Chazal regarding a certain matter, it may still leave room for one of the *mefarshim* to explain a *pasuk* in a way that differs from the way Chazal did. As an example, let us mention the famous explanation of Chazal concerning the passage in *Sefer*

---

95   See *Shabbat* 88b.

Devarim (26:5), "אֲרַמִּי אֹבֵד אָבִי," namely, that an *Arami* — Lavan — wanted to destroy my father — Yaakov. The **Ibn Ezra** raises a grammatical question on this explanation, the basis of which is that the word אֹבֵד is intransitive, that is, it refers to *the subject itself* being lost, not acting to destroy someone else. If the *pasuk* means to say that Lavan wanted to destroy Yaakov, it should have used the words מְאַבֵּד, which is transitive! Based on this question, the Ibn Ezra explains that the *pasuk* actually refers solely to Yaakov and is saying that "My father (Yaakov) was lost as an *Arami*," referring to the fact that Yaakov was never really successful or accepted in Aram. When the *pasuk* is read this way, we understand why it says "אֹבֵד," for it is saying that "*Avi*" — my father — was an "*Arami oved*" — a lost *Arami*.

This *peirush* of the Ibn Ezra is strongly contested by **R' Eliyahu Mizrachi**, who writes:

> *Chachameinu, z"l, transmitted this peirush based on their true kabbalah from an unbroken chain all the way back to Moshe Rabbeinu, alav hashalom, from Hashem Himself ("mipi ha'Gevurah") that the word "Arami" refers to Lavan, and that "oved" here is a transitive verb.*

Once again, we see that a *peirush* of the Ibn Ezra is attacked by one of the *mefarshim* on the basis of it conflicting with a *kabbalah* of Chazal. How would the Ibn Ezra respond to this? It appears that there are two options.

Firstly, it is possible that he would respond in a way similar to his position regarding Nimrod, i.e., that the words of Chazal here are not a *kabbalah*, but a *peirush*.

However, there is another possibility. Even if Ibn Ezra agrees that Chazal's words regarding Lavan were based on a *kabbalah*, it is possible that the *kabbalah* was **about Lavan**, i.e., that his true desire was to uproot and destroy Yaakov. However, that *kabbalah* does not necessarily relate to **the *pasuk*** of אֲרַמִּי אֹבֵד אָבִי, namely, that it is referring to Lavan trying to destroy Yaakov. Perhaps the truth about Lavan is known through *kabbalah*, and based on that Chazal themselves explained the *pasuk* as referring to that. To this, Ibn Ezra can reply, "I fully accept the **kabbalah** regarding Lavan's plans and motivations; however, I do not accept the **peirush** that Chazal gave to this particular *pasuk* in light of that *kabbalah*!"

An example of this second approach — of seeing a *kabbalah* as relating to an idea or person but not to the *peirush* of a *pasuk* — can be seen in the very words of the **Ramban** himself regarding Nimrod. On the one hand, Ramban criticizes the Ibn Ezra for portraying Nimrod in a positive light when we have a *kabbalah* from Chazal that he was a *rasha*. On the other hand, the Ramban himself explains the words of the *pasuk* that deal with Nimrod in a way that differs from Chazal. For, whereas Chazal explained the *pasuk* "הוּא הֵחֵל לִהְיוֹת גִּבֹּר בָּאָרֶץ" to mean that Nimrod brought the world to rebellion against Hashem, Ramban explains — *al derech peshuto* — that he was the first person to organize the conquest of another people. These words of the Ramban are quite remarkable. On the one hand, he criticizes the Ibn Ezra for explaining the *pesukim* that discuss Nimrod in a way that conflicts with the *kabbalah* of Chazal, and yet, in that very *parashah,* he proceeds to do exactly that!

We see clearly that the Ramban understood Chazal's *kabbalah* regarding Nimrod as one that relates to him, namely, that he was a *rasha.* This being the case, any *peirush* that portrays him in a positive light is in conflict with this *kabbalat Chazal*, and therefore unacceptable. However, although Chazal themselves then explained all of the *pesukim* that describe Nimrod in terms of his being a *rasha*, nonetheless, these *peirushim* themselves were not part of the *kabbalah*, and hence there is no objection to the Ramban explaining them in a way that differs from the *peirush* of Chazal — as long as his *peirush* is not in conflict with what we know from *kabbalat Chazal* about Nimrod as a person.

Knowledge of these *yesodot* will undoubtedly be of enormous value and benefit to the serious *lomed* as he makes his way through the *Chumash* with *Gedolei HaMefarshim.*

Ma'amar Nine

THE PAST TENSE AS PAST PERFECT IN
RASHI'S PEIRUSH

The Principle

IN THE BEGINNING of *perek* 4 of *Chumash Bereishit*, after describing the *chet* of Adam and Chavah and their banishment from Gan Eden, the Torah writes (*pasuk* 1):

וְהָאָדָם יָדַע אֶת חַוָּה אִשְׁתּוֹ

And Adam knew Chavah, his wife.

Commenting on these words, **Rashi** writes (s.v. *veha'adam*):

כְּבָר קוֹדֶם הָעִנְיָן שֶׁל מַעְלָה, קוֹדֶם שֶׁחָטָא וְנִטְרַד מִגַּן עֵדֶן, וְכֵן הַהֵרָיוֹן וְהַלֵּידָה. שֶׁאִם כָּתַב: "וַיֵּדַע אָדָם" – נִשְׁמָע שֶׁלְּאַחַר שֶׁנִּטְרַד הָיוּ לוֹ בָּנִים.

[This took place] already prior to the events mentioned above, before he sinned and was banished from Gan Eden, and so too with regards to the conception and birth of his sons. For had it written "va'yeda Adam," we would have understood that his sons were born after he was banished.

103

As if to say, whenever the Torah uses the (pure) past tense[96] instead of using the future (imperfect) tense with the *vav hahipuch* (*vav* conversive),[97] it means to imply the "past perfect," i.e., that this had **already** happened. This rule certainly makes sense in linguistic terms, since the pure past tense has no aspect of future tense in it. Therefore, since the Torah generally describes events by using the future tense and then reversing it with the *vav hahipuch*, should the Torah on occasion refer to a past event by using the past tense itself, with no future tense element, it would clearly imply an event that is "more in the past" than usual, i.e., that this had already happened.[98] This distinction has implications for many *pesukim* in the Torah. Indeed, the author of *Havanat HaMikra*, the great *medakdek* R' Zev Wolf Heidenheim, commented regarding this *klal* of Rashi, "Know this *klal* well, and keep it with you, for there are many places where you will need to make use of it."

Further Examples in Rashi

We find that Rashi himself frequently makes use of this *klal*, sometimes stating it explicitly, while other times making it clearly evident from his words. For example, later on in *Chumash Bereishit* (21:1), commenting on the words "וַה' פָּקַד אֶת שָׂרָה— *and Hashem re-membered Sarah*," Rashi writes (s.v. *va'Hashem*):

סָמַךְ פָּרָשָׁה זוֹ לְכָאן, לְלַמֶּדְךָ שֶׁכָּל הַמְבַקֵּשׁ רַחֲמִים עַל חֲבֵירוֹ
וְהוּא צָרִיךְ לְאוֹתוֹ דָּבָר, הוּא נַעֲנֶה תְּחִלָּה. שֶׁנֶּאֱמַר (לְעֵיל כ,יז):
"וַיִּתְפַּלֵּל...", וּסְמִיךְ לֵיהּ "וַה' פָּקַד אֶת שָׂרָה".

---

96   [E.g., the word אָמַר (he said).]

97   [E.g., taking the word יֹאמַר (he will say), and adding a letter *vav* to the beginning of the word — ויאמר (he said). It is worthwhile noting that when the *vav* functions as a *vav hahipuch*, it does not have the connotation of "and," which means the correct translation of the word "וַיֹּאמֶר" is "he said," and not "and he said."].

98   It is worthwhile noting that the use of a letter to change the future to the past and vice versa is something that has no parallel in any other language, but rather is unique to *Lashon HaKodesh*. A full discussion of this idea, however, is beyond the scope of this work.

The Torah juxtaposed this parashah to the preceding one[99]
to teach that one who asks for mercy on behalf of his fellow,
and he himself is in need of that very same thing, he will be
answered first, as it says, "he prayed etc.," and juxtaposed
to that, the pasuk "and Hashem remembered Sarah."

Rashi is explaining that the word *"pakad"* here, used in the past perfect tense, means that Hashem had already remembered Sarah prior to healing Avimelech. Indeed, Rashi in his *peirush* to *Bava Kama* (92a), which is the source of his comment here, states this explicitly: "מִדְּלָא כְּתִיב 'וַיִפְקוֹד אֶת שָׂרָה', וּכְתִיב 'פָּקַד', מַשְׁמַע פָּקַד כְּבָר תְּחִלָּה לַאֲבִימֶלֶךְ" — *from the fact that it does not say 'vayifkod et Sarah',[100] but rather said 'pakad',[101] the pasuk implies that He remembered her **before** (healing) Avimelech."*

Another example of Rashi basing himself on this principle without stating it explicitly can be found in his approach to the *sugya* of *Matan Torah* and the *Aseret HaDibrot*. The final *perek* of *Parashat Mishpatim* (*Shemot perek* 24), which is known as *Brit Torah*, is written after the *Aseret HaDibrot*, as well as after over fifty mitzvot of *Parashat Mishpatim*. Commenting on the opening words of that *perek*, Rashi writes:

וְאֶל מֹשֶׁה אָמַר עֲלֵה: פָּרָשָׁה זוֹ נֶאֶמְרָה קֹדֶם עֲשֶׂרֶת הַדִּבְּרוֹת,
וּבַד' סִיוָן נֶאֶמַר לוֹ 'עֲלֵה'.

And to Moshe He (Hashem) said, "Ascend." This parashah
was said before the Aseret HaDibrot; on the fourth of Sivan
he was told to ascend.

Rashi is clearly basing himself on the fact that the Torah uses the word *"amar"* (past perfect), and not *"vayomer el Moshe."* This comment has enormous ramifications regarding whether Bnei Yisrael saying

---

99   Describing Hashem's healing Avimelech and his household in response to Avraham's *tefilot* on their behalf.

100   [*Vav hahipuch.*]

101   [Pure perfect.]

"*Na'aseh V'Nishma*," the establishing of the *Brit* of Torah, the writing of the first "*megillah*" of Torah, and the offering of *korbanot* by the *bechorim*,[102] happened before the *Aseret HaDibrot* or afterward.

The Past Perfect in Halachah

It is important to note that the idea of the pure past tense denoting the past perfect exists not only in the narrative (*halichuti*[103]) sections of the Torah, but also in the sections dealing with halachah, for ultimately, the Torah is "one," i.e., consistent throughout. In the *parashah* of *Sotah*, the words "וְעָבַר עָלָיו רוּחַ קִנְאָה וְקִנֵּא אֶת אִשְׁתּוֹ" — *and a spirit of jealously passed over him and he warned his wife*" (*Bamidbar* 5:14) are written after "וְנִסְתְּרָה" — *and she was secluded*" (*pasuk* 13), even though the halachah states (and common sense dictates) that the warning precedes the seclusion and the questionable *tumah*. And, indeed, Rashi comments, "וְעָבַר עָלָיו, קוֹדֶם סְתִירָה" — *and a spirit [of jealously] passed over him **prior** to the seclusion*." In this case, Rashi is pointing out that the role of the *vav* at the beginning of the word "*v'avar*" is not that of *vav hahipuch* that changes the word from past to future tense, which would then be describing something that would have happened subsequently.[104] Rather, it is a *vav hachibur* (*vav* conjunctive), which simply means "and," leaving the rest of the word "*avar*" in the past perfect tense, and referring to the jealousy and warning that represent the first stage of the *Sotah* process.

In the *Acharonim*

The principle of past tense as past perfect is used by subsequent *mefarshim* as well. For example, **R' Yaakov Zvi Mecklenberg**, in his

---

102 [All of which are mentioned in *Shemot perek* 24.]

103 [The Rav had reservations about using the term "*sippuri*" when referring to the narrative *parshiyot* of the Torah, for he felt it has the connotation of "story — and no more." Therefore, he referred to these parts of Torah as "*halichuti*," indicating that while they are not halachic in nature, they do describe the "*halichot*" — the behavior — of those being spoken about and require us to learn from them regarding our own *halichot*.]

104 [I.e., "she was secluded" **and then** "a spirit of jealousy passed over him etc."]

peirush **HaKetav VeHakabbalah**, discusses the *parashah* of Yaakov buying Esav's *bechorah*, where a simple reading of the *pesukim* seems to indicate that Yaakov did not give Esav any food until he had sold his *bechorah*. Commenting on this understanding, Rav Mecklenburg writes (*Bereishit* 25:31, 34):

> *...According to this interpretation, you would be accusing Yaakov of something that is despicable even for a common person, who, when his brother comes in exhausted from the field and requests some food with which to restore his soul, does not give it to him right away, but rather waits until his hunger overpowers him and forces him to sell something against his will...is it the way of our Torah to speak in such a negative way about tzaddikim and inform future generations that they performed deeds that are objectionable?*
>
> *Rather, the evident truth is that it is not as those mefarshim describe. Lashon HaKodesh has two forms of referring to past events. The first is the future tense with the letter vav at the beginning, which denotes an event that happened then. The second form is the past perfect, which denotes something that had already happened earlier. Based on this established principle, you can see from the fact that the Torah does not say "*וַיִּתֵּן יַעֲקֹב*,"[105] but rather "*וְיַעֲקֹב נָתַן*,"[106] that Yaakov gave him food immediately upon his request and did not delay at all...*
>
> *And even though this[107] is written at the end [of the episode], it is possible to suggest a reason as to why it was not mentioned initially but rather delayed until the end, to teach us that Esav's disdain for the bechorah was not only at the [earlier] stage when he was tired and hungry, a decision that*

---

105 [*Vav hahipuch.*]
106 [Past perfect.]
107 [The Torah's mention of Yaakov giving food to Esav.]

he would perhaps regret later, after he had eaten. Rather, even after the entire episode was concluded, when he had already satisfied his hunger, his opinion did not change, for the whole idea of the bechorah was the subject of scorn in his eyes.[108]

Similarly, we find the Rav of Yerushalayim, **Maharil Diskin** (*Bereishit* 1:5), makes a most illuminating comment on the *pasuk* of "וַיִּקְרָא אֱלֹהִים לָאוֹר יוֹם וְלַחֹשֶׁךְ קָרָא לָיְלָה — *Hashem called light 'Day,' and darkness He called 'Night'*":

> *One may ask, why did the pasuk mention "day" before "night"? Does the pasuk itself not conclude by saying* "וַיְהִי עֶרֶב וַיְהִי בֹקֶר — *and it was evening and it was morning*" — *first darkness and then light! Additionally, the word* "קָרָא — *He called*" *seems redundant, for it could have said* "וַיִּקְרָא אֱלֹהִים לָאוֹר יוֹם וְלַחֹשֶׁךְ לָיְלָה — *Hashem called light 'Day,' and darkness 'Night'!*"
>
> *One may suggest the resolution to these questions based on Rashi's words later on, commenting on the pasuk (4:1)* "וְהָאָדָם יָדַע אֶת חַוָּה אִשְׁתּוֹ — *Adam knew his wife Chavah*" *that this took place prior to the above episode, before they had been banished from Gan Eden, for if this is something that happened subsequently, as indicated by the order of the pesukim, it should have written* "וַיֵּדַע אָדָם — *Adam knew*"... *Here too, the pasuk states* "וַיִּקְרָא אֱלֹהִים לָאוֹר יוֹם וְלַחֹשֶׁךְ קָרָא לָיְלָה — *Hashem called [using a vav hahipuch] the light 'Day' and darkness He called [past perfect] 'Night,'*" *indicating that the naming of "Night" had **already occurred** before the naming of "Day"! And the reason the pasuk did not mention these two things in the order they were named is because Hashem did not wish to associate His name with evil [darkness].*

---

108   [In other words, the Torah makes a point of juxtaposing Esav eating with the concluding words "וַיִּבֶז עֵשָׂו אֶת הַבְּכֹרָה — *and Esav scorned the bechorah*" in order to emphasize that his feelings toward it were deeply embedded and not just the product of hunger.]

She'eylat HaMadua

What is most interesting to note regarding these *peirushim* of *HaKetav VeHakabbalah* and *Maharil Diskin* is not only that they make use of Rashi's principle regarding past perfect, but that in their concluding words they both explain **why** the Torah wrote the earlier event later and then communicated through the use of the past perfect tense that it had already happened before. In the first case, it is to show the extent of Esav's disdain for the *bechorah*, and in the second, it is because "Hashem does not associate His name with evil."

In other words, the use of the past perfect tense may **inform** us that the action or event written later on in the Torah actually happened earlier; however, it does not **explain** why this is so. This second question falls within the realm of *"madua,"* and will require its own separate answer.

In this respect, our *sugya* of the Torah's use of the perfect tense is similar to that of אֵין מוּקְדָם וּמְאוּחָר בַּתּוֹרָה, which tells us that the order in which events are written in the Torah does not always reflect the chronological order in which they occurred. This principle is derived by the Gemara (*Pesachim* 7b) from the Torah itself, which states explicitly that the opening *perek* of *Chumash Bamidbar* happened a month **after** (*Rosh Chodesh Iyar*) the events described in *perek* 9 of *Bamidbar* (*Chodesh Nissan*). As such, all *mefarshim* agree regarding the existence of this *klal*. With regards to the question of when to apply it, however, the *Rishonim* differ greatly (Ramban — sparingly, Rashi — occasionally, the Ibn Ezra — frequently).

Here, too, we note that the *klal* of *"ain mukdam ume'uchar baTorah"* is merely identifying that the *parshiyot* **can** be written in non-chronological order. It does not, however, explain **why** this is so. The answer to that question must be based on some value that the Torah holds higher than the chronological order. If the Torah were there only to teach us history, then there could be no justification for presenting events out of order. However, since the words of the Torah teach us on the various levels of *pshat, drash, remez,* and *sod,* with each one making its contribution in revealing the will of the One Who gave us the Torah and how it obligates us, it should come as no surprise that the historical order can sometimes be pushed aside in favor of other requirements pertaining to what the Torah wishes to teach. As the *Be'er Yitzchak* (*Shemot* 32:31) puts it in his own unique way, "כִּי יֵשׁ סֵדֶר מוּקְדָּם לְסֵדֶר הַזְּמַנִּים — *for there is an order that takes precedence*[109] *over the order of events.*" This is why Rashi in his *peirush* to *Bamidbar perek* 9, having noted that the *parshiyot* are not in chronological order, proceeds to ask "וְלָמָּה לֹא פָּתַח בָּזוּ וכו' — *and why* did it not open with this [parashah]...?"[110]

Just as in cases of "*ain mukdam ume'uchar*," so too when we see verbs that are written in the past perfect and succeed in identifying that they are indeed out of chronological order, the next step is to ask "*madua*" and proceed to try and find out what additional message is behind this change as part of the *sheleimut* of Torah and its *kedushah*.

---

109 The Hebrew term here denoting taking precedence, "מוּקְדָּם," is a play on the words "אֵין מוּקְדָּם וּמְאוּחָר בַּתּוֹרָה."

110 I.e., *perek* 9. See *Kedushat Peshuto Shel Mikra*, *Parashat Terumah* for futher discussion.

Ma'amar Ten

MITZVOT AS
COMPOSITE ENTITIES

THE ISSUR OF cooking — and eating — meat and milk together appears three times in the Torah, twice in *Chumash Shemot* and once in *Chumash Devarim*. Let us pay careful attention to the way the *issur* appears in the Torah on the first two occasions, for only once we have succeeded in understanding the roots of this mitzvah and its essence, will we be able to appreciate the *chiddush* that occurs within it in *"Mishneh Torah"* — *Chumash Devarim*.

Basar B'chalav in *Chumash Shemot*

As we mentioned, this mitzvah appears for the first time in *Chumash Shemot* — a *Chumash* that does not contain any *perakim* dealing with foods that are or are not kosher.[111] It appears in the end of *Parashat Mishpatim* — a *parashah* that deals mainly with *sugyot* of *Choshen Mishpat*,[112] not *Yoreh De'ah*.[113] Specifically, it appears in

---

111 [It appears the Rav used the word *"perakim"* here with great precision, as there is a *pasuk* in *Parashat Mishpatim* that forbids *tereifah* (22:30). However, there are no **perakim** devoted to kosher foods, as there are in later *Chumashim*.]
112 [*Mitzvot* pertaining to money.]
113 [*Mitzvot* such as kashrut.]

conjunction with the *Shalosh Regalim* and *bikkurim*! The *pasuk* says (*Shemot* 23:19):

רֵאשִׁית בִּכּוּרֵי אַדְמָתְךָ תָּבִיא בֵּית ה' אֱלֹהֶיךָ לֹא תְבַשֵּׁל גְּדִי
בַּחֲלֵב אִמּוֹ:

The choice first fruit of your land you shall bring to the House of Hashem your God, you shall not cook a kid in its mother's milk.

This *pasuk* raises a number of issues in the area of *peshuto shel mikra*:

1. What does *basar b'chalav* have to do with *bikkurim*?
2. This *issur* is mentioned a second time in *Chumash Shemot* (34:26) in a *pasuk* that is completely identical to the first, i.e., a *lo taaseh* that is connected to *bikkurim*.
3. Moreover, it seems as if the only reason the mitzvah of *bikkurim* is mentioned in these *pesukim* is purely to serve as an introduction to the *issur* of *basar b'chalav*, since *bikkurim* has its own *parashah* in *Chumash Devarim* (*perek* 26). Indeed, that is the appropriate place for the mitzvah of *bikkurim*, since it does not apply until Eretz Yisrael has been conquered and divided up.
4. In both places in *Chumash Shemot* where this *issur* is mentioned, it is at the end of a *parashah* dealing with the *Shalosh Regalim*, and specifically in close proximity to *pesukim* that discuss the *issur* of *chametz* and the mitzvah of *korban pesach*.
5. The *issur* of *basar b'chalav* receives no mention — either explicit or otherwise — in what we would consider its "natural location," namely, the *parashah* of *ma'achalot asurim* in *Parashat Shemini*! Now, while it is true that in *Parashat Re'eh*, when it is mentioned for the third and final time, it does appear together with the other *ma'achalot asurim*, nonetheless, as we will see, even there it is not really **part** of the list, but rather seems to be **attached** to it.

6. The mentioning of the *issur* of *basar b'chalav* three times in the Torah is explained by Chazal as constituting three separate *issurim d'Oraita* with regards to meat and milk: cooking, eating, and deriving benefit. This seems quite difficult to understand. In what way is this *issur* more stringent than other "classic" nonkosher foods, such as pig, where there is an *issur* to eat them, but no additional *issur* to derive benefit from them, and certainly no *issur* to cook them?

That's quite a list!

The Essence of the *Issur* of *Basar B'chalav* — the Rambam's Approach

All these questions are dealt with and responded to by the classic *mefarshim*. For example, Rabbeinu Bachye (*Shemot* 23:19, s.v. *lo tevashel*) quotes the opinion of the **Rambam** in *Moreh Nevuchim* (3:48):

> *The Rambam provided a reason for this mitzvah in his discussion of ta'amei hamitzvot, that since it was the custom of idol worshippers to eat meat and milk when they performed their abominations during their festivals, therefore the Torah forbade it, and the pasuk says, "When **you** come to the House of Hashem, your God, during the shalosh regalim, do not cook a kid in its mother's milk as is the custom of idol worshippers." It is for this reason that this pasuk is written in two places within the context of the chagim, for this is the way of the Torah to forbid things that are part of the rituals of avodah zarah and to command us to do the opposite, in order to uproot avodah zarah and remove it from the world. This is what the Rav (Rambam), z"l, wrote as the reason for this mitzvah; even though these are not his words, this is his meaning.*

According to Rabbeinu Bachye's understanding of the Rambam's explanation, the basis of the *issur* of *basar b'chalav* is a certain form of *avodah zarah* rite. This explains why the *issur*, meant to distance us from those practices, is mentioned in the context of *avodat Hashem* in the *Beit HaMikdash* (*l'havdil!*). It is true that Chazal derived from these *pesukim* the many *halachot* that relate to the *issur* of *basar b'chalav*; nonetheless, we rely on Chazal as well regarding their statement that "*ain mikra yotzei midei peshuto*," that the *pshat* will always have something important to tell us about the mitzvah. Here, the *pshat* requires that we take note of the context in which the *issur* is written and leads us to conclude that in essence, *basar b'chalav* is rooted not in the *parashah* of *ma'achalot asurim*, but of *avodah zarah*. With this understanding we may answer questions 4 and 5 that we raised above.

The *Seforno* — *Basar B'chalav* and *Bikkurim*

Whereas the Rambam discussed the connection between "*lo tevashel*" and the *Mo'adim*, the **Seforno** (*Shemot* 23:19) deals with the connection between this mitzvah and the one mentioned in the beginning of the *pasuk*, namely, *bikkurim*:

> *Do not engage in those activities that are performed by idol worshippers in the belief that they will increase fertility; rather,* "רֵאשִׁית בִּכּוּרֵי אַדְמָתְךָ תָּבִיא בֵּית ה' אֱלֹהֶיךָ" — *the choice first fruit of your land you shall bring to the House of Hashem, your God," as the pasuk states elsewhere (Yechezkel 44:30),* "וְרֵאשִׁית כָּל בִּכּוּרֵי כֹל וְכָל תְּרוּמַת כֹּל מִכֹּל תְּרוּמוֹתֵיכֶם לַכֹּהֲנִים יִהְיֶה..." לְהָנִיחַ בְּרָכָה אֶל בֵּיתֶךָ — *all the first fruits of every species and all terumah of any kind of all your terumah shall be for the Kohanim...to place blessing within your home."*

According to the *Seforno*, the two halves of our *pasuk* make up one unifying message, with each half representing a positive and negative element respectively; if you wish to be recipients of Hashem's *berachah* in your endeavors, in the field, and so on, you should bring *bikkurim* to the *Beit HaMikdash* and not resort to activities such as cooking a kid in its mother's milk, which smack of the practices of those who believe in *avodah zarah*.

According to the *peirush* of the *Seforno* we can answer the first three questions that we raised above regarding the connection between *"lo tevashel"* and *bikkurim*. Moreover, not only do we understand why the *issur* of *"lo tevashel"* is written within the context of the *Mo'adim* generally and *bikkurim* specifically, we also understand why it was not written in its "natural" place, which is together with the *ma'achalot asurim* in *Parashat Shemini*. Both *bikkurim* and the *Mo'adim* serve to distance Am Yisrael from the rites of those who perform *avodah zarah*, and to show that it is Hashem who runs His world. The *Mo'adim* focus on Hashem's *hashgachah* of His people throughout world history, and *bikkurim* focuses on His supervision of the laws of nature as they express themselves in the agricultural cycle.

The Synthesis of *Pshat* and *Drash*

What emerges from the words of the Rambam, Rabbeinu Bachye, and the *Seforno* is that the *issur* of *"lo tevashel"* is rooted in the *sugya* of *hilchot avodah zarah*. This is in keeping with the role of *peshuto shel mikra*, even as the midrash performs its function and derives from these *pesukim* the *halachot* of the *issur* of *basar b'chalav*.

Moreover, we would like to suggest that not only is there no contradiction between the *pshat* and the midrash of these *pesukim*, but actually it is **only through the *pshat*** that we can fully understand some of the *halachot* of *basar b'chalav*, whose foundation lies within **the midrash** of the *pesukim*:

As we know, in halachah we do not generally make a *gezeirah* (protective measure) for another *gezeirah*,[114] yet when it comes to the *issur* of *basar b'chalav* we find no less than **four *gezeirot* — protective decrees**:

1. The *issur d'Oraita* applies only to eating meat of a *beheimah*[115] cooked in milk; Chazal applied it also to meat of a *chayah*,[116]

---

114   See, for example, Yerushalmi *Terumot* 9:1.
115   [Domesticated animals such as cattle and sheep.]
116   [Undomesticated animals such as deer.]

as a *gezeirah* to protect against a possible transgression concerning the *d'Oraita* of *beheimah*.

2. Chazal further forbade eating poultry cooked in milk.[117]
3. The *issur d'Oraita* applies only to eating meat and milk that were cooked together; Chazal extended the *issur* to eating them together even if they were not cooked together. This is also true for meat of a *chayah* and of poultry.
4. Even after eating meat, including meat of a *chayah* and poultry, we are required to wait a number of hours before eating milk products.

In no other area of *ma'achalot asurim* do we find anything even remotely like this! Why would Chazal here depart from the norm and apply this many *gezeirot* to *basar b'chalav* specifically, as opposed to, for example, the meat of a *chazir*?

Based on our approach, the matter is clear. When it comes to issues of *avodah zarah*, the *pasuk* states (*Devarim* 12:2), "אַבֵּד תְּאַבְּדוּן אֶת כָּל הַמְּקֹמוֹת אֲשֶׁר עָבְדוּ שָׁם הַגּוֹיִם — *you shall utterly destroy all the places where the nations worshipped*," upon which Chazal expounded (*Avodah Zarah* 45b), "מִכָּאן שֶׁצָּרִיךְ לְשָׁרֵשׁ אַחֲרֵי עֲבוֹדַת כּוֹכָבִים — *from here [we see] that we must eradicate any trace of avodah zarah*." Specifically in the area of *avodah zarah*, where there is a mitzvah to uproot any trace, we can understand why there would be room to enact a *gezeirah* to protect another *gezeirah* — and another one! And so, *peshuto shel mikra*, which reveals for us the *issur* of *basar b'chalav* as being rooted in *avodah zarah*, serves as the basis for understanding the unusual way in which Chazal related to the *halachot* of this mitzvah.

Basar B'chalav in Chumash Devarim

As we move from *Chumash Shemot*, where the first two mentions of *basar b'chalav* occur, to *Chumash Devarim*, where it is mentioned

---

117 [*Chayah* is much more similar to *beheimah* than is poultry, and hence, it would have been sufficient to prohibit *chayah* meat to protect the *issur d'Oraita* of *beheimah*. Nonetheless, Chazal extended the *issur* to poultry as well. The Rav sees this extension as a separate *gezeirah*.]

the final time, we sense a certain "change in direction"; the mitz-vah seems to detach itself from *bikkurim* and attach itself instead to its "natural" location, namely, the *halachot* of kashrut. The list in *Parashat Re'eh* of all the foods that we may or may not eat concludes with two additional *issurim* (14:21):

לֹא תֹאכְלוּ כָל נְבֵלָה... כִּי עַם קָדוֹשׁ אַתָּה לַה' אֱלֹקֶיךָ, לֹא תְבַשֵּׁל גְּדִי בַּחֲלֵב אִמּוֹ:

You shall not eat any neveilah[118]... for you are a holy nation unto Hashem your God, you shall not cook a kid in its mother's milk.

This is quite a remarkable situation. Initially, in *Parashat Shemini*, there was no mention whatsoever of *basar b'chalav* together with the other *ma'achalot asurim*, and now it has come to join them!

Yet, having noted the inclusion of *basar b'chalav* among the other *ma'achalot asurim*, if we look carefully at the above *pasuk* we will see that it doesn't seem to have been **completely** included in the list: The *pasuk* begins with the *issur* of *neveilah*, then says "כִּי עַם קָדוֹשׁ אַתָּה לַה' אֱלֹקֶיךָ," and then mentions the *issur* of *basar b'chalav*. However, the words "כִּי עַם קָדוֹשׁ וגו'" are essentially words of conclusion and summa-tion, and it is only after these words that the *pasuk* mentions *basar b'chalav*! Why would the *pasuk* conclude the list of *ma'achalot asurim* before mentioning everything that is on it?

Torat HaMurkavut — *Mitzvot* as **Composite Entities**

It appears that we have before us a wonderful example of "*Torat HaMurkavut*" regarding the mitzvot of the Torah, as we shall explain. A mitzvah is a composite entity, comprised of numerous different el-ements. Every mitzvah has a dominant element that determines the essence of the mitzvah. This element is analogous to the "head" or "heart" of the mitzvah. However, this does not mean that there are

---

118 [An animal that died through any means other than kosher *shechitah*.]

no other, secondary elements within the mitzvah, similar to a limb, or perhaps a finger.[119] The Netziv has explained to us in *Parashat Yitro* that every mitzvah contains within it details that are in the category of "*chok.*" However, that is only in relation to the primary reason for the mitzvah that is understood as a "*mishpat.*" According to our approach, we can understand why one cannot give a reason for the details of a mitzvah based on the reason for the mitzvah as a whole, for those details may represent a different element altogether. In our opinion, this is the deeper understanding of the Rambam's words (*Moreh Nevuchim* 3:36), that one cannot give reasons for the details of a mitzvah, and one who tries to do so "is engaged in one long delusion."

Dynamic Movement within Mitzvot

In this case we see that the mitzvah of "*lo tevashel*" has "moved" from the "family" of *avodah zarah* (in *Chumash Shemot*) to that of *ma'achalot asurim* (in *Chumash Devarim*). We have discussed elsewhere[120] that the *Seforno* has an approach, which we have called "לפני ואחרי — before and after," in which he contends that the mitzvot of the Torah changed, or in some cases were even introduced, as a result of the *Chet Ha'Egel* on the one hand, and the *Chet HaMeraglim* on the other. This is parallel to the way the laws of nature changed as a result of the *chet* of the generations of the *Mabul* and of *HaPalagah*, and primarily as a result of the *chet* of Adam HaRishon. Similarly, here, we would like to suggest that the function of the *issur* of *basar b'chalav* underwent a change as a result of the *chata'im* of Bnei Yisrael in the *Midbar*: of the *Egel*, the *Meraglim*, and the ten *nisyonot* with which they tested Hashem. In the same way as the *ma'achalot asurim* were introduced only after the spiritual decline that took place as a

---

119   In *Kedushat Peshuto Shel Mikra* this *sugya* is discussed in *Parashat Tetzaveh* and *Parashat Tzav.*

120   In *Kedushat Peshuto Shel Mikra* this topic is discussed in *Parshiot Shemini, Acharei Mot, Shelach* and *Pinchas.*

result of the *Chet Ha'Egel*,[121] so too a new type of *ma'achalot asurim* known as *basar b'chalav* was introduced as a result of the further spiritual decline that took place in the ensuing thirty-nine years. *"Lo tevashel"* left the category of *avodah zarah* and entered the category of *ma'achalot asurim*. Before the period of the forty years in the *Midbar*, the dominant element within the mitzvah was that of *avodah zarah*, with the element of *ma'achalot asurim* possibly joining it in a secondary capacity. Now, at the end of the forty years, with Bnei Yisrael having tested Hashem on numerous other occasions, the element of *avodah zarah* stepped down from its dominant position, and in its place came the element of *ma'achalot asurim*. Therefore, at this point it is appropriate for it to be mentioned in a list together with the other *ma'achalot asurim*.

We note that the situation with *"lo tevashel"* is a little different than that of the *ma'achalot asurim* of *Parashat Shemini*. In their case, the *issur* itself was introduced — according to the *Seforno* — as a result of *chet*, so that something that was previously permissible to eat is now forbidden. In the case of *"lo tevashel,"* what has been introduced is not the fact that it is *assur* to eat — which it already was — but rather the essence and function of this *issur*, for it has moved from one area of *issurim d'Oraita* to another. It seems clear that the problem of *avodah zarah* was greater immediately upon leaving Mitzrayim — the world center of *avodah zarah* — than it was forty years later, since Bnei Yisrael witnessed *hashgachah pratit* on a level of which the world had never seen or heard (the *Mann*, water from Miriam's Well, the *Ananei HaKavod*, and so on). As Bnei Yisrael are just about to enter Eretz Yisrael, the dominant theme is no longer *avodah zarah,* but recognizing the direct *hashgachah* of Hashem.

If it were possible to apportion one hundred points to every mitzvah in the Torah, we might say that in the period of *Parashat Mishpatim*, the mitzvah of *"lo tevashel"* was comprised of eighty

---

121   As the *Seforno* explains. The *Seforno's* approach is discussed in *Kedushat Peshuto Shel Mikra*, in *Parashat Shemini*.

percent *issur avodah zarah* and twenty percent *ma'achalot asurim*. Now, in *Chumash Devarim*, as they are about to enter Eretz Yisrael, the internal composition has shifted, so that eighty percent is now of *ma'achalot asurim* and only twenty percent is of *avodah zarah*. We should emphasize, and we will presently see, that the element of *avodah zarah* did not disappear altogether, but became diminished and assumed secondary status within the mitzvah.

Included, Yet Distinct

This brings us back to the point mentioned before. The sensitive eye that observes carefully the way the Torah is written will note that the transition from *avodah zarah* to *ma'achalot asurim* is not complete — the *issur* of *"lo tevashel"* never became an integral part of the list of *ma'achalot asurim*. Not only does it appear at the very end of the list, from a certain point of view it is not on the list at all! The section of *ma'achalot asurim* concludes with the wonderful words "כִּי עַם קָדוֹשׁ אַתָּה לַה' אֱלֹקֶיךָ" — *for you are a holy nation unto Hashem your God.*" *Ma'achalot asurim* are certainly connected with the *kedushah* of Am Yisrael. Why, then, is the *issur* of *basar b'chalav* left on "the other side of the fence," after the words "עַם קָדוֹשׁ וגו'"?

Evidently, although a change has taken place in the function of the mitzvah of *"lo tevashel,"* it is not a total change. While it is true that it is no longer **primarily** connected to *bikkurim* or *avodah zarah*, but rather to *ma'achalot asurim*, nonetheless, it still retains a secondary element of avoiding *avodah zarah* rites. The way the Torah communicates this significant — but not total — transition is to move this mitzvah to the *parashah* of *ma'achalot asurim*, but then to "formally" conclude that *parashah* before mentioning it. This informs us that it has not been fully absorbed in the new *parashah*; rather, it still contains elements of the "root mitzvah," *avodah zarah*, as indeed we noted above that Chazal applied "a *gezeirah* to a *gezeirah*" in keeping with the *avodah zarah* element within the mitzvah that still remains.

Reverberations in Rashi

The unusual way in which the Torah listed *"lo tevashel"* in *Parashat Re'eh* was also noted by *"Parshandata"* — that is, Rashi.[122] The following section in the *parashah* opens with "עַשֵּׂר תְּעַשֵּׂר," the mitzvah of taking *maaser* from produce in the field. **Rashi** comments:

מַה עִנְיָן זֶה אֵצֶל זֶה, אָמַר לָהֶם הקב״ה לְיִשְׂרָאֵל לֹא תִּגְרְמוּ לִי
לְבַשֵּׁל גְּדָיין שֶׁל תְּבוּאָה עַד שֶׁהֵן בִּמְעֵי אִמּוֹתֵיהֶן, שֶׁאִם אֵין אַתֶּם
מְעַשְׂרִים מַעַשְׂרוֹת כָּרָאוּי, כְּשֶׁהוּא סָמוּךְ לְהִתְבַּשֵּׁל אֲנִי מוֹצִיא
רוּחַ קָדִים וְהִיא מְשַׁדַּפְתָּן.

What does one matter have to do with the other? Said Hashem to Yisrael, "Do not cause Me to 'cook' the young grain while it is still in its 'mother's womb.' For if you do not take maasrot properly, I will produce an easterly wind when the grain is about to ripen, which will scorch it."

The *Be'er Yitzchak*[123] explains that the scorching of the grain while it is still on its stalk through an easterly wind is the equivalent of cooking it while it is still "with its mother." In order to teach that this punishment will occur for one who does not take *maasrot* properly, the Torah juxtaposed the mitzvah of *maasrot* with that of "cooking a kid in its mother's milk."

However, the entire matter seems problematic from the outset! Why did Rashi see fit to comment on the juxtaposition of the *parashah* of *basar b'chalav* with that of *maasrot*? We have been taught a *klal gadol* by the greatest of the *Mefarshei Rashi*, R' Eliyahu Mizrachi, regarding Rashi's approach in his *peirush* on the Torah — namely, that he will only comment on *semichut haparshiyot* (juxtaposed sections) if that *semichut* appears in conflict with *peshuto shel mikra*. Yet in our

---

122 [The term פרשנדתא as a reference to Rashi, which the Rav used frequently, was coined by the Ibn Ezra in his Introduction to his *peirush* on the Torah. In this context the term is as a contraction of the words "פרשן דתא — the (quintessential) commentator of the Torah."]

123 A classic commentary on *Peirush Rashi* by R' Yitzchak Hurwitz of Jaroslaw, Poland.

case there does not seem to be any difficulty in the juxtaposition of a section dealing with food that is *assur* to eat (*basar b'chalav*) and one of commanding how to render food permissible to eat (*maasrot*). This being the case, what problem did Rashi see here in *peshuto shel mikra* that caused him to comment on the *semichut*?

However, based on our discussion, the matter is readily understood. Rashi is responding to the very point that we mentioned earlier — that the *issur* of "*lo tevashel*" was not placed together with the other *ma'achalot asurim*, but rather was mentioned after the concluding words "כִּי עַם קָדוֹשׁ אַתָּה." Rashi is bothered by the fact that this mitzvah was seemingly "removed" from being inside the *parashah* and was placed on the outside! To this Rashi responds by saying that the intention of the Torah was not to remove it from the first *parashah*, but rather to connect it to the following *parashah* of *maasrot*, in order to teach us the lesson that Rashi proceeds to quote.[124]

Rashi's Concluding Words

Moreover, if this approach is correct, it will also help us understand the final three words of Rashi, which we did not mention until now, "וְכֵן לְעִנְיַן בִּכּוּרִים — *and so too with regards to bikkurim*," i.e., this punishment of the grain being scorched while in its stalks will also occur with one who withholds *bikkurim*. At first glance, these words are utterly astounding; who brought *bikkurim* into this discussion? It is not the way of Rashi to teach us *halachot* that are not relevant to the issue at hand! Here, the two matters being spoken about are "*lo tevashel*" and *maasrot*. Why does Rashi feel the need to "enlighten us" regarding the additional halachah of *bikkurim* when it has no direct bearing on the discussion at hand? The matter becomes even more difficult when we notice that in the source of Rashi's comment, the Midrash Tanchuma, there is no mention of *bikkurim* whatsoever!

---

124 Based on the *sefer Maskil L'David* on *peirush* Rashi. We should note that it is possible to suggest that there is more leeway to be *doresh semichut haparshiyot* in *Chumash Devarim* than in the earlier *Chumashim*; see our discussion in *Parashat Devarim* (*Kedushat Peshuto Shel Mikra*) regarding the nature of *Chumash Devarim*.

However, with our approach, the words of Rashi are "a delight for the eyes." While *"lo tevashel"* has found its place among the *ma'achalot asurim* in *Sefer Devarim*, it has not totally shed its original *avodah zarah* element. That element remains, albeit to a diminished degree. It is this dual essence of the mitzvah that allows it to be placed on the "other side" of the words "כִּי עַם קָדוֹשׁ אַתָּה" without violating its integrity as one of the *ma'achalot asurim*. Given that this element remains, if *semichut haparshiyot* teaches us that not taking *maasrot* can lead to a punishment along the lines of "a kid in its mother's womb," then this will certainly be the case if one does not bring *bikkurim*, for that mitzvah was bound up with *"lo tevashel"* from the outset, and the essential connection between them remains! Hence, Rashi's concluding words "and so too with regards to *bikkurim*."

It is appropriate to mention here that the *peirush* **Levush Ha'Orah** on Rashi, which is the only one among the classic *Mefarshei Rashi* who addresses the problem that we raised, may have had our understanding in mind when he wrote, *"And so too regarding bikkurim, and it is for this reason the Torah juxtaposed, both in Parashat Mishpatim and in Parashat Ki Tisa, the words 'lo tevashel gedi' with the words 'reishit bikkurei admat'cha.'"*

This appears to be the way to explain the words of Rashi within the context of the *sugya* in its totality. May Hashem grant us illumination in the study of His Torah.